The People of ABERDEEN

at Home and Abroad

1800-1850

By David Dobson

CLEARFIELD

Copyright © 2022
by David Dobson
All Rights Reserved

Published for Clearfield Company by
Genealogical Publishing Company
Baltimore, Maryland
2022

ISBN: 9780806359434

Introduction to People of Aberdeen, 1800-1850

From the medieval period until the Victorian era, Aberdeen was comprised of two separate burghs, Old Aberdeen and New Aberdeen. Old Aberdeen was centred on St Machar's Cathedral when King David I established a new bishopric there around 1125. That settlement became a burgh of barony in 1489. New Aberdeen, a burgh since 1214, was an important regional market town and port, exporting locally produced wool, woolfells, hides and fish, and importing flax, timber, iron, grain, wine, spices, and luxury goods. Its burgesses traded with England, the Low Countries, France, and the Baltic. The two burghs in Aberdeen each had their own burgh council, burgess roll, court, college and other institutions that maintained their own records--some of which have been published by the Spalding Club in Aberdeen.

The two burghs merged in the mid nineteenth century to establish a unified city. For example King's College, founded in Old Aberdeen in 1495, and Marischal College, founded in New Aberdeen in 1593, united in 1860 to form the University of Aberdeen. Aberdeen became the major city in north-east Scotland with its economy based on the aforementioned industries together with shipbuilding, whaling, herring fishing, woollens especially stocking-making, and papermaking.

This book contains references to people from Aberdeen at home and abroad, between 1800 and 1850. The entries bring together emigrants, their destinations, especially in North America, the West Indies, and Australasia, with their kin who remained in Scotland. The information is derived from a wide range of sources such as court records, contemporary newspapers and journals, monumental inscriptions, and documents found in archives. The Statistical Report of Scotland (O.S.A.), compiled between 1791 and 1799; and the New Statistical Report, conducted between 1832 and 1845, are especially helpful for understanding the rapid changes in Scottish society brought about by the Agricultural and Industrial Revolution during this period. This should enable researchers with roots in Aberdeen to put their family into a historical context.

David Dobson

Dundee, Scotland, 2022

REFERENCES

ACA   Aberdeen City Archives

AH   Aberdeen Herald, series

AJ   Aberdeen Journal, series

ANQ   Aberdeen Notes and Queries, series

ANY   St Andrew's Society of New York

AP   St Andrew's Society of Philadelphia

AR   Acadian Recorder, series

BA   Officers of the Bengal Army

BPP   British Parliamentary Papers, series

DCB   Dictionary of Canadian Biography

DPCA   Dundee, Perth,& Cupar Advertiser

EA   Edinburgh Advertiser

EEC   Edinburgh Evening Courant, series

F   Fasti Ecclesiae Scoticanae

GA   Greenock Advertiser, series

GM   Gentleman's Magazine, series

IJ   Inverness Journal, series

KCA   King's College Aberdeen

LCL   Leith Commercial Lists, series

MCA   Marischal College, Aberdeen

MG   Montreal Gazette, series

NARA   National Archives, Records Administration

NRS National Records of Scotland

OD Scots in the Old Dominion

PANS Public Archives of Nova Scotia

POD Post Office Directory

QC Quebec Courier, series

QM Quebec Mercury, series

SAA Society of Advocates in Aberdeen

TNA The National Archives

WC Weekly Chronicle, series

Castle Street, Aberdeen

King's College, Aberdeen

Old Aberdeen

Town House and New Inn, 1822, Aberdeen

Old and West Churches

Gordon's Hospital

THE PEOPLE OF ABERDEEN, AT HOME AND ABROAD, 1800-1850

ABEL, PETER, son of Peter Abel in Aberdeen, was educated at Marischal College in 1843 and graduated MD from King's College, Aberdeen, on 18 April 1845. [MCA][KCA]

ABERCROMBY, ANDREW, born 1843, late of the Northern Insurance Company in Aberdeen, died in New York on 3 July 1872. [AJ.31.7.1872]

ABERCROMBIE, JOHN, late Provost of Aberdeen, died there on 9 June 1820. [AJ.9.6.1820] [SM.86.190]

ADAM, ELIZABETH, wife of Joseph Almond an iron-turner in Ship Row, Aberdeen, was accused of housebreaking and theft in 1822. [NRS.AD14.22.130]

ADAMSON, DAVID, from Aberdeen, a general agent in Gray Town, married Anna Christina Margaret Scheepers, daughter of Gent Scheepers in Uitenhage, Cape Colony, in Gray Town, Port Natal, South Africa, on 25 March 1864. [AJ.6078]

ADDISON, ALEXANDER, born 1759, educated in Aberdeen, a minister in Pennsylvania, by 1785, a lawyer in Washington County, Pa., from 1787, a Judge from 1790 to 1803, died in Pittsburgh, Pa., on 27 November 1807. [AP]

AIKEN, JAMES BURNETT, son of James Aiken a missionary from Aberdeen, was educated at Marischal College, Aberdeen, in 1852, later was a sugar planter in Natal, South Africa. [MCA]

AITKEN, ISABELLA CAROLINE, youngest daughter of Reverend Roger Aitken, late Rector of St John's, Lunenburg, Nova Scotia, formerly in Aberdeen, died in Fredericton, New Brunswick, on 14 January 1848. [AJ.5223]

AITKEN, WILLIAM FERGUSON, son of Reverend John Aitken in Aberdeen, graduated MA from Marischal College in 1847, a minister in Glasgow. [MCA]

ALCOCK, Reverend ALEXANDER, graduated MA from Trinity College in Dublin, in 1770, Episcopal minister of St Paul's Chapel from 1793, died in Aberdeen in 1807. [AJ.29.2.1807]

ALCOCK, JAMES, a medical student in Aberdeen, was accused of violating sepulchres in 1812. [NRS.AD14.12.58]

ALEXANDER, THOMAS, born 1805, son of James Alexander and his wife Margaret Crombie in Aberdeen, educated at King's College, Aberdeen, 1820-1824, graduated MA from Marischal College, a minister in Cobourg, Canada. [KCA][MCA]

ALLAN, ALEXANDER, was admitted as a cabinetmaker burgess of Old Aberdeen on 28 October 1865. [ACA]

ALLAN, ANN, daughter of Robert Allan in Aberdeen, a master in the Royal Navy, married Robert McBeth of St John, New Brunswick, there on 14 June 1827. [CG.20.6.1827]

ALLAN, ELIZA, daughter of Captain George Allan of Links Street, Aberdeen, married John Leslie, a watchmaker in Bytown, Canada West, in Montreal on 7 October 1851. [AJ.5418]

ALLAN, GEORGE, a merchant, was admitted as a burgess of Old Aberdeen on 28 September 1801. [ACA]

ALLAN, G., master of the <u>Sarah of Aberdeen</u> from Aberdeen with passengers bound for Quebec in 1842. [AH.23.4.1842]

ALLAN, ISABELLA, wife of John Paterson an advocate, died in Aberdeen in 1842. [AJ.30.12.1842]

ALLAN, JEAN, a prisoner in Aberdeen Tolbooth, was sentenced to transportation beyond the seas, on 20 September 1800. [NRS.JC11.44]

ALLAN, or KNOX, JEAN, in New Brunswick, heir to her grandfather Arthur Gibbon a shipowner in Aberdeen, 1837; also, to her aunts Isabella Gibbon and Christian Gibbon in Aberdeen. [NRS.S/H]

ALLAN, JOHN, born 1786 in Aberdeen, an apothecary, died in St John, New Brunswick, on 17 September 1825. [NBC.24.9.1825]

ALLAN, JOHN, son of George Allan sr., was admitted as a burgess of Old Aberdeen on 6 October 1836. [ACA]

ALLAN, PETER, was admitted as a brickmaker burgess of Old Aberdeen on 26 October 1812. [ACA]

ALLAN, R., master of the Thistle of Aberdeen bound for Quebec, with passengers in 1821 and 1822. [QM][MG]

ALLAN, WILLIAM, a merchant in Aberdeen, died 27 July 1848, father of Peter Duncan Allan, a mariner in Chewton, Victoria, Australia. [NRS.S/H]

ALLARDYCE, GEORGE, son of Andrew Allardyce in Aberdeen, graduated MA from Marischal College, Aberdeen, in 1794. [MCA]

ALLARDYCE, JAMES, son of William Allardyce a wine merchant in Aberdeen, was educated at Marischal College in 1844, a Colonel of the Madras Staff Corps, Honourable East India Company Service. [MCA]

ALLATHAN, JAMES, was admitted as a trade burgess of Old Aberdeen on 1 November 1819. [ACA]

ALLISON, JOHN, and his wife Mary Ann Simpson, were parents of James Allison, born 1856, died in New York on 19 January 1890, husband of Jessie Smith. [St Clement's gravestone, Aberdeen]

ALVES, WILLIAM, son of William Alves a weaver in Aberdeen, graduated MA from Marischal College in 1843, later a Presbyterian minister in New Brunswick. [MA]

AMSLEY, ALEXANDER, born 1776 in Aberdeen, a mariner, applied to be naturalised in South Carolina on 24 July 1804. [NARA.M1183.1]

ANDERSON, ALEXANDER, was admitted as a blacksmith burgess of Old Aberdeen on 25 January 1802. [ACA]

ANDERSON, ALEXANDER, of Bourtie, born 1745, died in Aberdeen in 1825. [AJ.21.3.1825]

ANDERSON, ALEXANDER, master of the Carlton of Aberdeen from Aberdeen with passengers bound for Quebec in 1835 and in 1838. [QM]

ANDERSON, ALEXANDER, from Old Machar, Aberdeen, was educated at King's College in 1848, later a schoolmaster. [KCA]

ANDERSON, ALEXANDER, son of Reverend Alexander Anderson in Old Aberdeen, was educated at Marischal College in 1848, later an employee of the Oriental Bank in Melbourne, Victoria, Australia. [MCA]

ANDERSON, ALEXANDER, was admitted as a merchant burgess of Old Aberdeen on 31 October 1825. [ACA]

ANDERSON, ANDREW, was admitted as a blacksmith burgess of Old Aberdeen on 18 May 1801. [ACA]

ANDERSON, ARCHIBALD EDMONSTON, son of John Anderson a merchant in Aberdeen, graduated MA from Marischal College in 1848, a licentiate of the Free Church of Scotland. [MCA]

ANDERSON, GEORGE, jr., was admitted as a tailor burgess of Old Aberdeen on 15 February 1814. [ACA]

ANDERSON, GEORGE, was admitted as a merchant burgess of Old Aberdeen on 22 December 1823. [ACA]

ANDERSON, HANNA, born 1837 in Aberdeen, died in Nova Scotia in 1928. [Palmerston gravestone, Pugwash, Cumberland County, N.S.]

ANDERSON, JAMES, was admitted as a merchant burgess of Old Aberdeen on 8 October 1808. [ACA]

ANDERSON, JAMES, was admitted as a trade burgess of Old Aberdeen on 26 October 1818. [ACA]

ANDERSON, JAMES, born 1743, former master of Robert Gordon's Hospital, died in Aberdeen in 1822. [AJ.16.11.1822]

ANDERSON, JAMES, a merchant in Sydney, Cape Breton, Noa Scotia, accounts re the St Andrew of Aberdeen, master William Penn, 1842. [AUL.2295/1-2]

ANDERSON, JOHN, was admitted as a merchant burgess of Old Aberdeen on 1 October 1804. [ACA]

ANDERSON, JOHN, wood-sawyer, Gallowgate, parish of St Nicholas, Aberdeen, a victim of crime in 1825. [NRS.JC26.1825.29]

ANDERSON, JOHN, son of William Anderson a merchant in Aberdeen, graduated MA from Marischal College in 1840, later in America. [MCA]

ANDERSON, MARGARET, born 1757, spouse of Peter Gill a watchmaker, died in Aberdeen in 1828. [AJ.11.12.1828]

ANDERSON, MARY, daughter of John Anderson in Old Aberdeen, married John Steven Holmwood in Woolwich, Upper Canada, on 14 March 1837. [AJ.4660]

ANDERSON, ROBERT, master of the Sir William Wallace of Aberdeen from Aberdeen with passengers bound for Miramachi, New Brunswick, in 1829 and 1833. [DPCA]

ANDERSON, Captain, master of the Quebec Packet of Aberdeen from Aberdeen with passengers bound for Quebec in 1829; master of the Helen of Aberdeen from Aberdeen with passengers bound for Quebec in 1832. [AJ][QM]

ANDERSON, WILLIAM, was admitted as a trade burgess of Old Aberdeen on 30 October 1820. [ACA]

ANDERSON, WILLIAM GEORGE, in USA, son and heir of Jean Jamieson, wife of James Anderson a shoemaker in Denburn, Aberdeen, 1860. [NRS.S/H]

ANDERSON, WILLIAM TORRY, in Aberdeen, died 15 October 1863, brother of Thomas Gordon Anderson in Collendina, New South Wales, Australia. [NRS.S/H]

ANDREWS, A., master of the Sir William Wallace of Aberdeen from Aberdeen with passengers bound for Quebec in 1855. [QM]

ANDREW, JAMES, born 1773 in Aberdeen, Principal of the Honourable East India Company Military Seminary at Addiscombe, died in Edinburgh in 1833. [AJ.13.6.1833]

ANGUS, ALEXANDER, born 1720, a book seller in Aberdeen, died in 1802. [AJ.21.9.1802]

ANGUS, GEORGE, born 12 October 1794, son of Reverend Alexander Angus and his wife Katherine Mair in Botriphnie, a physician in the Honourable East India Company Service, died in Aberdeen on 7 April 1872. [F.6.302]

ANGUS, HENRY, son of Reverend Henry Angus in Aberdeen, graduated MA from Marischal College in 1848, later a United Presbyterian minister. [MCA]

ANGUS, JOHN, born 1743, a bookseller in Aberdeen, died in 1828. [AJ.15.10.1828]

ANGUS, ROBERT, son of Reverend Henry Angus in Aberdeen, graduated MA from Marischal College in 1845, later a United Presbyterian minister in Peebles. [MCA]

ANGUS, WILLIAM, of Montego Bay Jamaica, son of Alexander Angus a bookseller in Aberdeen, died at sea off Port Antonio in February, 1807. [DPCA.267] [SM.69.798]

ANGUS, Mrs, born 1751, widow of Reverend Alexander Angus in Botriphnie, died at 74 Dee Street, Aberdeen. [AJ.26.10.1836]

ANNAND, Reverend ADAM, born 1779, Episcopalian minister of St John's Chapel, died in Aberdeen in 1818. [AJ.1.4.1818]

ANNAND, HELEN, daughter of John Annand of Belmont, Aberdeen, and wife of Walter Learmonth, died in London in 1832. [AJ.17.8.1832]

ANNAND, JOHN SHAND, son of Robert Annand a weaver in Aberdeen, was educated at Marischal College in 1847. [MCA]

ANNAND, WILLIAM, born 1804 in Aberdeen, died at Lower Stewiacke, Nova Scotia, on 7 July 1833. [Acadian Recorder, 13.7.1833]

ANSON, JAMES, a boy in the Poor Hospital, son of the late David Anson a horsehirer, was apprenticed to Peter Elmslie a shoemaker in Aberdeen from 1787 to 1793. [ACA]

ARGO, ALEXANDER, born 1789, a surgeon, died in Aberdeen in 1841. [AJ.5.9.1841]

ARTHUR, BARBARA, eldest daughter of James Arthur in King Street, Aberdeen, married Alexander Smith of Annapolis County, Nova Scotia, in Halifax, N.S., on 28 June 1848. [AJ.5246]

ARTHUR, JAMES, was admitted as a merchant burgess of Old Aberdeen on 8 October 1808. [ACA]

ARTHUR, JOHN, eldest son of James Arthur, was admitted as a blacksmith burgess of Old Aberdeen on 14 November 1835. [ACA]

ARTHUR, WILLIAM, son of Reverend Michael Arthur in Aberdeen, a minister in Edinburgh 1790, in Glasgow in 1793, and in Pequa, Pennsylvania before 1818, died there in 1827. [UPC]

ARTHURSON, SCOTT, was admitted as a trade burgess of Old Aberdeen on 29 October 1821. [ACA]

AULDJO, GEORGE, born 1756, late Provost of Aberdeen, died in Aberdeen in 1806. [AJ.24.11.1806]

BAIN, JAMES, son of Farquhar Bain a flax-dresser, was apprenticed to William Bean a weaver in Aberdeen from 1789 to 1796. [ACA]

BAIN, JOHN, was educated at King's College, Aberdeen, in 1820, later was a minister and author in Galt, Ontario. [KCA]

BAIN, WILLIAM, agent of the City of Glasgow Bank in Aberdeen in 1849. [POD]

BALMANNO, ROBERT, in Brooklyn, New York, heir to his sister Helen Balmanno in Aberdeen, 1857. [NRS.S/H]

BANNERMAN, Sir ALEXANDER, of Kirkhill, MD, born 1741, died at his house in Marischal Street, Aberdeen, in 1813. [AJ.29.12.1813]

BANNERMAN, ALEXANDER, baptised on 16 January 1786 in Aberdeen, son of Charles Bannerman and his wife Margaret Wilson, a soldier from 1804 to 1825, a Captain of the 20th Native

Infantry of the Bengal Army, married Penelope Smith in Cawnpore India, in 1822, died in Arakan, Burma, on 19 July 1825. [BA.I.88]

BANNERMAN, CHARLES, born 1750, an advocate, died in Aberdeen in 1813. [AJ.24.9.1813]

BANNERMAN, GEORGE, son of Thomas Bannerman a merchant in Aberdeen, was educated at Marischal College, Aberdeen, in 1840s. [MCA]

BANNERMAN, JOHN, son of John Bannerman a mason in Aberdeen, was apprenticed to Robert Smith a merchant in Aberdeen, from 1788 to 1791. [ACA]

BANNERMAN, THOMAS, born 1795, a manufacturer, died at 263 Union Street, Aberdeen, in 1843. [AJ.14.4.1843]

BANNERMAN, WILLIAM, son of Patrick Bannerman an advocate in Aberdeen, was educated at Marischal College in 1842, later in the Service of the Honourable East India Company. [KCA]

BARCLAY, ALEXANDER, MD, born 1810, died in Newburgh, New York, on 1 May 1889. [St Clement's gravestone, Aberdeen]

BARNES, or HUNTER, in Aberdeen, died on 22 April 1868, mother of George Hunter in Massourie, Upper India. [NRS.S/H]

BARNET, GEORGE, from Aberdeen, died in Lockport, Will County, Illinois, on 5 January 1861. [AJ.5913]

BARNET, LEWIS, born 1773 in Aberdeen, died in Lockport, Illinois, in 1856. [AJ.12.11.1856][S.20952]

BARRACK, GEORGE, was admitted as a mason burgess of Old Aberdeen on 3 October 1832. [ACA]

BARRACK, JOHN, eldest son of William Barrack, was admitted as a burgess of Old Aberdeen on 14 November 1825. [ACA]

BARRACK, JOHN, from Old Machar, Aberdeen, was educated at King's College, Aberdeen, in 1847, later a minister. [KCA]

BARRACK, WILLIAM, born 1790, was admitted as a burgess of Old Aberdeen on 8 October 1808. [ACA]; a merchant in Old Aberdeen, died in 1843. [AJ.23.7.1843]

BARRON, GEORGE, born 1800, son of John Barron a watchmaker in Aberdeen, a Writer to the Signet, died at 83 Crown Street, Aberdeen, in 1851. [AJ.11.8.1851]

BARRON, JOHN, born 1810 in Aberdeen, son of John Barron, [1765-1852], and his wife Ann Allan, of 83 Crown Street, a watchmaker who died in New York on 30 August 1851. [AJ.5408] [Old Machar gravestone]

BARSTOW, FRANCES, born 1769, daughter of Thomas Barstow in Leeds, and niece of Sir Alexander Bannerman of Elsick, died in Dee Place, Aberdeen, in 1832. [AJ.7.1.1832]

BARTLET, JOHN, was admitted as an upholsterer burgess of Old Aberdeen on 26 October 1812. [ACA]

BARTLET, THOMAS, was admitted as an upholsterer burgess of Old Aberdeen on 26 October 1812. [ACA]

BARTLET, Captain, master of the Earl of Hopetoun of Aberdeen from Aberdeen to Sydney, Cape Breton, Nova Scotia, in 1844. [LCL]

BATE, GERARD, was admitted as a blacksmith burgess of Old Aberdeen on 24 April 1827. [ACA]

BAXTER, ANDREW JAMES BURT, son of Reverend Daniel Burt in Aberdeen, was educated at Marischal College in 1849, later a minister. [MCA]

BAXTER, JOHN, a fisherman in Footdee in 1793. [NRS.S/H]

BEATTIE, ALEXANDER, born 1815, with Christina Beattie, born 1817, and John Beattie, born 1840, arrived in Kingston, Jamaica, on 11 May 1841 on board the Rob Roy from Aberdeen. [TNA.CO140/33]

BEGG, ALEXANDER, master of the Venus of Aberdeen from Aberdeen with passengers bound for Quebec in 1813. [NRS.E504.1.24]

BEGG, CHARLES, born 1825, a pianoforte maker from Aberdeen, died in Dunedin, Otago, New Zealand, on 24 January 1875. [AJ.6633]

BEGG, JOHN, born 4 April 1825, son of Alexander Begg, [1750-1825], and his wife Elspet Riddle, [1757-1845], died in New Orleans, Louisiana, on 7 August 1858. [St Peter's, Spittal, Aberdeen, gravestone]

BENTLEY, JANET, wife of William Littlejohn a banker in Aberdeen, died there in 1848. [AJ.1.10.1848]

BERNIE, WILLIAM, born 1782 in Aberdeen, a merchant in Charleston, South Carolina, was naturalised there on 29 September 1806. [NARA.M1183.1]

BERRY, JOHN, from Aberdeen, [brother of James Berry a gardener and riddlemaker at North Broadford, Aberdeen], arrived in Quebec from Chicocoutimie on 8 June 1840.

BEST, ALEXANDER VANS, son of Thomas Best a silversmith in Aberdeen, was educated at Marischal College in 1849. [MCA]

BEST, ALEXANDER VANS, son of Thomas Best a silversmith in Aberdeen, was educated at Marischal College in 1849. [MCA]

BEST, THOMAS, agent of the British Linen Company in Aberdeen in 1849. [POD]

BEST, WILLIAM JAMES, son of Thomas Best a banker in Aberdeen, was educated at Marischal College in 1850s, later a merchant in Bombay, India. [MCA]

BEVERLEY, ALEXANDER, son of Alexander Beverley in Aberdeen, was educated at Marischal College in 1840. [MCA]

BEVERLEY, JAMES, son of Andrew Beverley, was apprenticed to James Simpson a tailor in Aberdeen from 1784 to 1791. [ACA]

BEVERLEY, JOHN, son of Alexander Beverley a tailor, was admitted as a wright burgess of Old Aberdeen on 21 April 1800. [ACA]

BEVERLEY, JOHN, was admitted as a baker burgess of Old Aberdeen on 2 November 1807. [ACA]

BEVERLEY, Captain, master of the Lion of Aberdeen from Aberdeen to Quebec on 11 April 1860. [AJ]

BIRD, JAMES, from Aberdeen, graduated MA from King's College, Aberdeen, on 31 March 1814, later the Physician General of the East India Company. [KCA]

BIRNIE, ALEXANDER, son of Alexander Birnie a stonemason in Aberdeen, was educated at Marischal College in 1846. [MCA]

BIRNIE, ALEXANDER, Commander of the Ann Duthie of Aberdeen married Grace Marshall, daughter of Allan A. Marshall of Bon Accord Works, Macquarrie Place, Sydney, late of Aberdeen, in Sydney, New South Wales, Australia, on 28 October 1869. [AJ.6366]

BIRNIE, GEORGE, born 1778 in Aberdeen, a merchant in Charleston, South Carolina, was naturalised there on 19 October 1818. [NARA.M1183]

BIRNIE, JOHN, born 1787 in Aberdeen, a millwright in Charleston, South Carolina, was naturalised in October 1828. [NARA.M1183]

BIRNIE, PETER, born 1792 in Aberdeen, died 25 August 1819. "came to this country to join his brothers William, John, and George". [Old Third Presbyterian gravestone, Charleston, South Carolina.]

BIRNIE, WALTER, born in Aberdeen, a cooper in Quebec for twenty-five years, died there on 19 September 1849. [AJ.5312]

BIRNIE, WILLIAM, in Aberdeen, nephew and heir to William Black in Charleston, South Carolina, 1835. [NRS.S/H]

BIRSS, ROBERT, a wholesale druggist in Aberdeen, father of Robert Birss jr, born 1857, died in Georgetown, Demerara, on 3 June 1884. [AJ.9.6.1884]

BISSET, DAVID, son of James Bisset, Court House, Aberdeen, died in Huntingdon, America, in 1869. [AJ.28.7.1869]

BISSETT, ISABELLA, eldest daughter of William Bissett in Aberdeen, married R. Crossley of South Bridge, Massachusetts, in Birmingham on 10 June 1858. [W.XIX.1989]

BISSET, JAMES, born 1843, son of William Bisset in Upper Kirkgate, Aberdeen, died in Grenada on 10 May 1865. [AJ.21.6.1865]

BISSET, PATRICK DUFF, born 1823 in Aberdeen, died in Liberty, Texas, on 19 October 1860. "shot by a drunken man whom he had expelled from his house"; his son, Patrick Duff Bisset died there on 20 June 1860; another son Walter Scott Bisset died there on 1 November 1860. [AJ.28.11.1860]

BISSET, JAMES, a watchmaker in Aberdeen, father of William Bisset who graduated MA in 1858 and MD in 1861, settled in Queenstown, Cape Colony, South Africa. [MCA]

BLACK, ELIZABETH, born 1751, widow of James Young a merchant in Aberdeen, died there in 1836. [AJ.8.5.1836]

BLACK, GEORGE WATSON, born 1796, son of Thomas Black and his wife Margaret Innes in Aberdeen, was educated at King's College, Aberdeen, from 1809 to 1813, emigrated to America. [KCA]

BLACK, JAMES, was admitted as a trade burgess of Old Aberdeen on 26 October 1818. [ACA]

BLACK, JAMES, son of James Black a merchant in Aberdeen, a student at Marischal College in 1830s, later a Major General of the Bombay Army. [MCA]

BLACK, JOHN, born 1763, from Aberdeen, a merchant in St John, New Brunswick, later in Halifax, Nova Scotia, died at Summer Hill, Aberdeenshire, on 4 September 1823, probate, Halifax, Nova Scotia, 1823. [New Machar gravestone]

BLACK, JOHN, born 1752 in New Machar, died in Charleston, South Carolina, on 11 September 1834, a resident for sixty years. [AJ.22.10.1834]

BLACK, THOMAS, son of William Black a merchant in Aberdeen, graduated MA from Marischal College in 1818, later a merchant in Batavia, Java, Dutch East Indies. [MCA]

BLACK, THOMAS ROBERTSON, formerly a butcher in New Market, Aberdeen, died at Alma Goldfield, Australia, on 17 September 1855. [AJ.5647]

BLACK, WILLIAM, born 1760, died in Aberdeen in 1833. [AJ.26.9.1833]

BLACKIE, GEORGE WEST, son of Alexander Blackie a silversmith in Aberdeen, was educated at Marischal College in 1843, later an actor. [MCA]

BLACKIE, JAMES HAMILTON, son of Alexander Blackie a banker in Aberdeen, died off the coast of Chile in 1851. [AJ.5398] [W.1232]

BLAIKIE, ANTON ADRIAN, son of James Blaikie an advocate, was educated at Marischal College in 1842, later an advocate. [MCA]

BLAIKIE, JAMES, son of John Blaikie a plumber in Aberdeen, was educated at Marischal College in 1845. [MCA]

BLAIKIE, JOHN, son of Dr Patrick Blaikie in Aberdeen, was educated at Marischal College in 1850, later a missionary in New Zealand. [MCA]

BLAIKIE, JOHN, son of David Blaikie a plumber in Aberdeen, was educated at Marischal College in 1842, later an iron-founder in Aberdeen. [MCA]

BLAIKIE, PATRICK, MD, a surgeon in the Royal Navy, and physician at the Aberdeen Lunatic Asylum, died in Aberdeen in 1830. [AJ.27.2.1830]

BLAKE, GEORGE BANNERMAN, son of James Blake in Aberdeen, was educated at Marischal College in 1845, later a minister. [MCA]

BODDIE, ALEXANDER, son of John Boddie in Aberdeen, was educated at Marischal College in 1840. [MCA]

BOGART, DAVID BROWN, in Prossiac, New Jersey, heir to his grand-aunt Margaret Lamond in Aberdeen, who died in January 1833. [NRS.S/H]

BONNYMAN, JAMES, son of James Bonnyman a blacksmith in Aberdeen, was educated at Marischal College in 1845. [MCA]

BOOTH, JAMES, son of John Booth a blacksmith in Aberdeen, was apprenticed to Alexander Booth a merchant there from 1787 to 1792. [ACA]

BOOTH, JOHN, was admitted as a blacksmith burgess of Old Aberdeen on 18 May 1801. [ACA]

BOOTH, JOHN, born 1771, founder of the 'Aberdeen Chronicle', and a magistrate there, died in Aberdeen in 1849. [AJ.12.7.1849]

BOOTH, JOHN, son of John Booth a clockmaker in Aberdeen, was educated at Marischal College in 1848, later a writer in Aberdeen and in Edinburgh. [MCA]

BOOTH, JOSEPHINE, in Aberdeen, versus her spouse William Launie, a Lieutenant of the 26th Regiment, a Process of Separation, 1815. [NRS.CC8.6.1566]

BOOTH, LIVINGSTONE, born 1780, a merchant and shipowner in Aberdeen, died in Dundee in 1836. [AJ.29.1.1836]

BOOTH, ROBERT, a shipmaster in Aberdeen, husband of Isobel Smith in 1793. [SPEBR]

BOTHWELL, JOHN, a mariner in Old Aberdeen in 1796. [ROA.I.375]

BOTHWELL, WILLIAM, in Aberdeen, a Lieutenant of the Royal Navy, testament, 1822, Comm. Aberdeen. [NRS]

BOW, ANN, daughter of Thomas Bow a merchant in Aberdeen, married George Laing from Winchester, Upper Canada, in Montreal, Quebec, on 14 October 1836. [AJ.4637]

BOWER, JOHN, born 1750, late teacher in Aberdeen, died in 1820. [AJ.8.11.1820]

BOWIE, JOHN HENRY, born 1807, son of William Bowie in Aberdeen, emigrated to New York in 1825, a leather merchant there, a Member of the Legislature 1847-1848, married Mary Jane Busby, died in Brooklyn, N.Y., on 3 July 1859. [ANY][AJ.3.8.1859]

BOYD, JANE, born 1766, wife of James Kidd the Professor of Oriental Languages at Marischal College, Aberdeen, died in 1829. [AJ.4.6.1829]

BRAND, Mrs GEORGE, from Aberdeen, died in Lexington, Kentucky, on 5 September 1849. [AJ.5313]

BRAND, JAMES, born 1744, Cashier to the Aberdeen Banking Company, died in Aberdeen in 1825. [AJ.18.8.1825]

BRANDS, MARION, youngest daughter of James Brands of Ferryhill, died in Aberdeen in 1821. [AJ.18.5.1821]

BREBNER, ALEXANDER CROMBIE, son of James Crombie an advocate in Aberdeen, was educated at Marischal College in 1847, later in Somerset House, London. [MCA]

BREBNER, ARCHIBALD, born 1770 in Aberdeen, a merchant tailor, was naturalised in South Carolina on 16 May 1805. [NARA.M1183.1]

BREBNER, CHRISTIAN, born 30 September 1847 in Aberdeen, wife of Alexander Fettes, died in South Africa on 23 August 1916. [St George gravestone, Port Elizabeth, Cape of Good Hope, South Africa]

BREBNER, GEORGE HAMILTON GORDON, son of James Brebner an advocate in Aberdeen, was educated at Marischal College around 1850, later settled in Australia [MCA]

BREBNER, JAMES, son of James Crombie an advocate in Aberdeen, was educated at Marischal College in 1849. [MCA]

BREBNER, JOHN, was found guilty of libel and sentenced to transportation to the colonies for 7 years, at Aberdeen in 1813. [NRS.GD1.959]

BRENNAN, JAMES, born 1817, with Margaret Brennan, born 1823, and Margaret Brennan, born 1841, arrived in Kingston, Jamaica, on 11 May 1841 on board the Rob Roy from Aberdeen. [TNA.CO140/33]

BRENNER, JOHN, born 1805, with Isabella Brenner, born 1807, John Brenner, born 1835, Elspeth Brenner, born 1837, and Jane Brenner, born 1839, arrived in Kingston, Jamaica, on 11 May 1841 on board the Rob Roy from Aberdeen. [TNA.CO140/33]

BRENNER, JOSEPH, born 1823, arrived in Kingston, Jamaica, on 11 May 1841 on board the Rob Roy from Aberdeen. [TNA.CO140/33]

BRODIE, Mrs FLORA, born 1831 in Aberdeen, wife of John Brodie, died in San Francisco, California, on 8 September 1873. [San Francisco Morning Call, 9.9.1873]

BRODIE, FRANCIS, was admitted as a tailor burgess of Old Aberdeen on 25 February 1814. [ACA]

BRODIE, JAMES, a pilot in the Royal Navy, testament, 1814, Comm. Aberdeen. [NRS]

BRODIE, JOHN, born 1819, son of John Brodie, [1787-1865], and his wife Mary Walker, [1786-1846], died in Quebec on 5 September 1846. [St Clement's gravestone, Aberdeen]

BRODIE, THOMAS, from Aberdeen, a factor in Charleston, South Carolina, probate, 27 July 1798, S.C.

BROWN, ALEXANDER, born 1802, third son of Alexander Brown of the Inland Revenue in Aberdeen, died at Kent Cottage, Balmain, Sydney, New South Wales, Australia, on 29 January 1874. [AJ.6587]

BROWN, ALEXANDER, a bookseller and former Provost of Aberdeen, died there in 1848. [AJ.17.11.1848]

BROWN, ALEXANDER, in Aberdeen, died 8 January 1862, father of Mary Brown or Arnold in Lafayette, Rhode Island. [NRS.S/H]

BROWN, ALEXANDER, born 1843 in Aberdeen, a soldier of the US Cavalry in 1876. [S]

BROWN, BENJAMIN, born 1851, youngest son of Peter Brown an auctioneer in Aberdeen, died in Naseby, Otago, New Zealand, on 22 August 1875. [AJ.6667]

BROWN, DAVID, a weaver and broker in Aberdeen, was accused of theft in Dundee in 1823. [NRS.AD14.23.165]

BROWN, GEORGE, was admitted as a tailor burgess of Old Aberdeen on 23 January 1832. [ACA]

BROWN, GEORGE, son of John Brown a shoemaker in Aberdeen, was educated at King's College in 1854. [KCA]

BROWN, JAMES, born 1797, son of William Brown a book-seller in Aberdeen, was educated at Marischal College, Aberdeen, graduated MA in 1815, minister of the Scots Church in Calcutta, India in 1821, died in Malacca, Malaya, on 23 September 1830. [F.7.570] [MCA]

BROWN, Dr JAMES, a physician in Aberdeen, died in Old Aberdeen in 1838. [AJ.2.8.1823]

BROWN, JOHN, from Aberdeen, graduated MA from King's College, Aberdeen, in March 1820, later a minister of the Scots Kirk in Rotterdam, Zealand. [KCA]

BROWN, JOHN MOORE, fourth son of Dr W. L. Brown the Principal of Marischal College, Aberdeen, died in Hamilton, Upper Canada, on 19 August 1849. [AJ.5307] [SG.1858]; heir to his sister Helen Brown, 1849. [NRS.S/H]

BROWN, PETER, sr., born 1767, an auctioneer, died in Aberdeen in 1838. [AJ.26.3.1838]

BROWN, P., from Aberdeen, husband of Mary Mackay who died in Fergus, Nichol township, Upper Canada, on 20 November 1839. [AJ.4801]

BROWN, ROBERT, born 1811, an advocate in Aberdeen, died in 1848. [AJ.12.3.1848]

BROWN, Reverend WILLIAM LAURENCE, Professor of Divinity, Principal of Marischal College, minister of the West Church, Dean of the Chapel Royal, and Chancellor of the most Ancient Order of the Thistle, died in Aberdeen in 1830. [AJ.11.5.1830]

BROWN, WILLIAM, 1807-1887, and his wife Helen McMillan, 1810-1872, in Aberdeen, grandparents of James Black jr., born 1871, in Oakland, California, on 21 June 1904. [St Peter's gravestone, Spittal, Aberdeen]

BROWN, ..., master of the whaling ship Dee of Aberdeen bound via Stromness and Lerwick for Greenland in 1820. [EEC.16987]

BROWNING, Reverend WILLIAM, jr., born 1792, minister of St Andrew's Chapel, died in Aberdeen in 1843. [AJ.29.5.1843]

BRUCE, JAMES, son of William Bruce in Aberdeen, was educated at Marischal College in 1846. [MCA]

BRUNTON, ELIZA, eldest daughter of John Brunton a shipmaster in Aberdeen, married Ronald C. MacFie from London, Canada West, in Boston, USA, on 3 November 1862. [AJ.5993]

BRYCE, Reverend JOHN, born 1754, minister of the South Parish of Aberdeen, died in 1831. [AJ.10.12.1831]

BUCHAN, ALEXANDER, born 1788, a harpooner in Peterhead, was drowned in the wreck of the whaling ship Oscar of Aberdeen in 1813. [AJ]

BUCHAN, GEORGE, was admitted as a trade burgess of Old Aberdeen on 26 October 1818. [ACA]

BUCHAN, GEORGE, born 1784, a harpooner in Peterhead, drowned in the wreck of the whaling ship Oscar of Aberdeen in 1813. [AJ]

BUCHAN, THOMAS, of Auchmacoy, born 1746, died in Old Aberdeen in 1819. [AJ.12.8.1819]

BURN, GEORGE ALEXANDER, son of Edward Burn a gentleman in Aberdeen, was educated at Marischal College, in 1848. [MCA]

BURNETT, ALEXANDER, a merchant in Aberdeen, brother of William Burnett, a sailor in Philadelphia, Pennsylvania, 1793. [NRS.S/H]

BURNETT, ANN, wife of George Marquis an accountant, died at 16 Albyn Place, Aberdeen, in 1849. [AJ.28.2.1849]

BURNETT, ARTHUR, son of William Burnett an advocate in Aberdeen, died in Jamaica on 22 May 1794. [SM]

BURNETT, ELIZABETH, born 1745, daughter of George Burnett of Caskieben, died in Aberdeen in 1816. [AJ.27.3.1816]

BURNETT, JAMES G., of Friendville, Aberdeen, married Mary Grace Tyrel, youngest daughter of Nathan Tyrel of Providence, Rhode Island, in New York in 1837. [AJ.4683]

BURNETT, or STRACHAN, MARGARET, in America, heir and niece of Alexander Burnett, a weaver in Old Aberdeen, 1840. [NRS.S/H]

BURNET, PETER, a provincial land surveyor in Canada West, son and heir of Elizabeth Tower or Burnet, widow of Francis Burnet in Aberdeen, 1865. [NRS.S/H]

BURNETT, THOMAS, son of Alexander Burnett a gardener in the Hardgate of Aberdeen, was apprenticed to William Seaton a baker in Aberdeen from 1785 to 1790. [ACA]

BURNETT, THOMAS, a writer in Aberdeen, son of William Burnett an advocate in Aberdeen, was admitted as a Notary Public on 7 March 1795, died 1 December 1854. [NRS.NP2.35.239]

BURNET, WILLIAM, a chaise driver in Aberdeen, later a sailor on the sloop of war Delight, testament, 1792, Comm. Edinburgh. [NRS]

BURNET, WLLIAM, a sailor in Philadelphia, Pennsylvania, heir to his brother Alexander Burnet a merchant in Aberdeen, in 1793. [NRS.S/H]

BURR, GEORGE, was admitted as a merchant burgess of Old Aberdeen on 31 October 1814. [ACA]

BURT, JOHN, a shipmaster in Aberdeen in 1790. [NRS.S/H]

BYERS, WILLIAM, a goldsmith in Aberdeen, died in 1811, testament, 24 October 1811, Comm. Aberdeen. [NRS]

CADENHEAD, ALEXANDER, a shipmaster in Aberdeen, testament, 1794, Comm. Aberdeen. [NRS]

CADENHEAD, ALEXANDER S., son of Alexander Cadenhead an advocate in Aberdeen, was educated at Marischal College in 1840, emigrated to Canada. [MCA]

CADENHEAD, GEORGE, son of Alexander Cadenhead an advocate in Aberdeen, was educated at Marischal College in 1841, later became the Procurator Fiscal of Aberdeen. [MCA]

CADENHEAD, JAMES, son of Alexander Cadenhead an advocate in Aberdeen, was educated at Marischal College in 1841, joined the Merchant Navy [MCA]

CADENHEAD, JOHN, was admitted as a gardener burgess of Old Aberdeen in November 1811. [ACA]

CADENHEAD, JOHN, son of John Cadenhead a gardener in Aberdeen, was educated at Marischal College in 1820s, later was a surgeon in the Service of the East India Company. [MCA]

CADENHEAD, JOHN, son of Alexander Cadenhead an advocate in Aberdeen, graduated MA from Marischal College in 1839, later a farmer in Ontario and an Inspector of Schools. [MCA]

CADENHEAD, WILLIAM, son of Robert Cadenhead, was apprenticed to Peter Robertson a staymaker in Aberdeen from 1782 to 1787. [ACA]

CAIE, ROBERT, son of Robert Caie a brickmaker in Old Aberdeen, was apprenticed to John Nicoll an ironmonger in Aberdeen, from 1787 to 1791. [ACA]

CALDENHEAD, GEORGE, was admitted as a tailor burgess of Old Aberdeen on 12 February 1854. [ACA]

CALDER, JAMES, born 1745, a wine merchant, died in Aberdeen in 1832. [AJ.10.9.1832]

CALDER, JOHN, in the Poor Hospital, son of the late William Calder a tailor, was apprenticed to Donald McDonald a tailor in Aberdeen from 1790 to 1796. [ACA]

CALDER, WILLIAM, was admitted as a tailor burgess of Old Aberdeen on 3 February 1859. [ACA]

CAMERON, MARY, born 1789, a widow in North Street, Aberdeen, was accused of uttering forged notes in 1824. [NRS.AD14.24.89]

CAMERON, DONALD, born 1808, a sawyer, arrived in Kingston, Jamaica, on 11 May 1841 on board the Rob Roy from Aberdeen. [TNA.CO140/33]

CAMPBELL, ALEXA, in Aberdeen, versus Malcolm Gillespie an Excise officer, in 1814. [NRS.CC8.6.1543]

CAMPBELL, DUNCAN, a surgeon in Honourable East India Company Service at Fort Marlborough, Sumatra, East Indies, father of Margaret, testament, 1796, Comm. Aberdeen. [NRS]

CAMPBELL, GEORGE, son of Alexander Campbell a baker in Aberdeen, was educated at Marischal College in 1849, later a minister. [MCA]

CAMPBELL, JOHN, born 1792, a cooper from Aberdeen, emigrated to New York aboard the brig Gowan in September 1822. [NARA]

CAMPBELL, JOHN CHARLES, son of John Campbell Carr in Aberdeen, was educated at Marischal College in 1848. [MCA]

CAMPBELL, JOHN MITCHELL, born 1797, late surgeon on Honourable East India Company Service, died at 5 Golden Square, Aberdeen, in 1848. [AJ.3.2.1848]

CAMPBELL, WILLIAM, son of John Campbell a surgeon in Aberdeen, a student at Marischal College in 1840s, later the British Consul in Finland. [MCA]

CAMPBELL, W., Vice Consul of Stettin, second son of Dr John Campbell in Aberdeen, married Emily Cook, second daughter of C. J. Cook in Essex late of Madras, India, in the British Vice Consulate in Stettin, Prussia, on 15 August 1854. [W.XV.1576]

CARGILL, Captain JOHN, master of the Kingston of Aberdeen from Aberdeen with passengers bound for Quebec in 1837 and 1838. [AJ]

CARNEGIE, JOHN WILLIAM, born 21 April 1814 in Aberdeen, son of David Carnegie, a surgeon in Bombay, India, and his wife Anne, a soldier from 1832 to 1862, a Major of the Bengal Army, married Jane Scott in Calcutta in 1838, died in England on 6 January 1874. [BA.I.306]

CARNEGIE, JOHN, from Aberdeen, was educated at King's College, Aberdeen, in 1857, a physician in China. [KCA.308]

CARNEGIE, WILLIAM, a writer in Edinburgh, son of Alexander Carnegie the town clerk of Aberdeen, was admitted as a Notary Public on 31 May 1794, died on 28 May 1840. [NRS.NP35.155]

CARR, GEORGE, son of Robert Carr a merchant in Aberdeen, was educated at Marischal College in 1848. [MCA]

CARTER, CHARLES, of Galena, born 1823, son of David Carter in Aberdeen, died at his brother's house in Chicago, Illinois, on 14 July 1860. [AJ.1.8.1860]

CARTER, JAMES, son of David Carter a blacksmith in Aberdeen, was educated at Marischal College from 1831 to 1835, graduated MA, a banker and merchant in St Louis, Missouri, and in Chicago, Illinois. [MCA]

CASSIE, ALEXANDER, a skipper in Aberdeen, husband of Margaret McAllan, testament, 1818, Comm. Aberdeen. [NRS]

CASSIE, JAMES, a prisoner in Aberdeen Tolbooth, was banished from Scotland for seven years on 16 April 1796. [NRS.JC11.42]

CASSIE, JOHN, was educated at King's College, Aberdeen, in 1805, a minister of the Dutch Reformed Church at Caledon, South Africa, from 1828 to 1850. [F.7.561]

CASSIE, JOHN, from Aberdeen, graduated MA from King's College in 1827, later a minister in Port Hope, Ontario, Canada. [KCA]

CASSIE, JOHN, from Aberdeen, graduated MA from King's College in 1827, later a minister in Port Hope, Ontario, Canada. [KCA]

CATTERNICH, Mrs CHARLOTTE ADELAIDE, widow of Captain William Catternich from Aberdeen, married William Millard, from Bristol, in Halifax, Nova Scotia, on 24 July 1842. [AR:30.7.1842]

CATTO, JOHN, son of William Catto a merchant in Aberdeen, was educated at Marischal College in 1848, later a shipbroker in Aberdeen. [MCA]

CATTO, ROBERT, born 1772, a merchant and shipowner, died in Aberdeen in 1854. [AJ.3.11.1854]

CHALMERS ALEXANDER WALLACE, son of Alexander Wallace in Aberdeen, was educated at Marischal College in1843, later a chief engineer of the Royal Navy. [MCA]

CHALMERS, ALEXANDER HENDERSON, son of Charles Chalmers an advocate in Aberdeen, was educated at Marischal College in 1845, later a Writer to the Signet. [MCA]

CHALMERS, CATHERINE, born 1770, widow of Provost Alexander Brown, died at 158 King Street, Aberdeen, in 1850. [AJ.11.6.1850]

CHALMERS, GEORGE, was admitted as a trade burgess of Old Aberdeen on 13 November 1802. [ACA]

CHALMERS, JAMES, from Aberdeen, was educated at King's College, Aberdeen, in 1806, a minister in the West Indies. [KCA]

CHALMERS, JAMES HAY, son of Charles Chalmers an advocate in Aberdeen, was educated at Marischal College in 1842, later an advocate in Aberdeen. [MCA]

CHALMERS, JAMES HAY, son of Charles Chalmers an advocate in Aberdeen, was educated at Marischal College in 1842, later an advocate in Aberdeen. [MCA]

CHARLES, GEORGE, was admitted as a burgess of Old Aberdeen on 10 April 1813. [ACA]

CHARLES, GEORGE, jr., was admitted as a merchant burgess of Old Aberdeen on 22 December 1823. [ACA]

CHARLES, GEORGE, sr., was admitted as a merchant burgess of Old Aberdeen on 22 December 1823. [ACA]

CHEYNE, EUPHEMIA, born 1788 in Aberdeen, youngest daughter of Alexander Cheyne, wife of James Johnston, died on Waverley farm, Stanford township, Drummondville, Upper Canada, on 10 September 1838. [AJ.4737][SG.714]

CHEYNE, PETER, son of Peter Cheyne a merchant in New Machar, was educated at Marischal College in 1841. [MCA]

CHEYNE, WILLIAM ANNAND, son of Patrick Annand an Episcopalian minister in Aberdeen, graduated MA from Marischal College in 1841. [MCA]

CHISHOLM, ALEXANDER, was admitted as a burgess of Old Aberdeen on 8 October 1808 [ACA]

CHISHOLM, GEORGE, born in Aberdeen, a mariner who fought at the Battle of Camperdown, died in Buenos Ayres, Argentina, in 1830, brother of Mr Chisholm the architect. [AJ.17.11.1830]

CHISHOLM, JAMES, was admitted as a merchant burgess of Old Aberdeen on 8 October 1808 [ACA]

CHIVAS, ALEXANDER, born 1764, late cashier of the Commercial Banking Company, died in Aberdeen in 1844. [AJ.24.1.1844]

CHRISTIE, ALEXANDER, son of Alexander Christie a merchant in Aberdeen, was educated at King's College, Aberdeen, in 1812, later in the service of the Hudson Bay Company. [KCA]

CHRISTIE, HELEN, from Aberdeen, married Robert Hendrie, in San Francisco, California, on 29 September 1856. [AJ.5680]

CHRISTIE, ISABELLA, widow of Principal McLeod of Old Aberdeen, a petition, 1820. [NRS.CC12.6.9.2]

CHRISTIE, JOHN, born 1836 in Aberdeen, died in Wynberg, Cape of Good Hope, South Africa, on 8 October 1864. [AJ.6102]

CHRISTIE, MARY J., wife of Francis William Stafford a painter in New York, heir to her grandmother, Mary Diack, wife of George Christie in Aberdeen, 1859. [NRS.S/H]

CLARK, ALEXANDER, was admitted as a shoemaker burgess of Old Aberdeen on 29 October 1821. [ACA]

CLARK, ALEXANDER, son of John Clark, was admitted as a cooper burgess of Old Aberdeen on 26 October 1835. [ACA]

CLARK, ALEXANDER, was admitted as a shoemaker burgess of Old Aberdeen on 25 October 1856. [ACA]

CLARK, AMELIA, daughter of Lieutenant Colonel Clark in Aberdeen, married John Ogilvy Moffatt, eldest son of George Moffatt, in Montreal, Quebec, on 6 August 1844. [AJ.5045]

CLARK, DAVID, born 1806, a shipmaster who died in New Orleans, Louisiana, on 22 November 1854. [St Clement's gravestone, Aberdeen]

CLARK, GEORGE, born 1778, a bookseller, died at 2 Guest Row, Aberdeen, in 1849. [AJ.19.1.1849]

CLARK, GEORGE, was admitted as a baker burgess of Old Aberdeen on 1 October 1835. [ACA]

CLERK, JAMES, born 1749, son of John Clerk of Kincardine, died in Aberdeen in 1829. [AJ.9.4.1829]

CLARK, GEORGE, son of Alexander Clark a writer in Aberdeen, educated at Marischal College in 1841, died when a student. [MCA]

CLERK, JAMES, son of Gilbert Clerk a mason from Aberdeen then in Jamaica, with consent of Isobel Gauld his mother, was apprenticed to Charles Lunan a clock and watchmaker in Aberdeen from 1779 to 1788. [ACA]

CLARK, JAMES, was admitted as a tailor burgess of Old Aberdeen on 24 April 1854. [ACA]

CLARK, JOHN S., from Old Machar, educated at King's College in 1847, later a minister. [KCA]

CLARK, ROBERT, son of James Clark, was admitted as a painter burgess of Old Aberdeen on 12 February 1854. [ACA]

CLARK, WILLIAM, son of George Clark a tailor, was apprenticed to William and James Christie, saddlers in Aberdeen, from 1790 to 1796. [ACA]

CLARK, WILLIAM MORTIMER, son of John Clark in Aberdeen, a student at Marischal College in 1850s, was admitted as a Writer to the Signet in 1859, later a barrister in Ontario. [MCA]

CLYNE, HELEN GOLDIE, in Cleveland, Ohio, heir to her grandfather William Clyne a leather merchant in Aberdeen who died on 14 October 1843. [NRS.SH]

CLYNE, JAMES, a leather merchant from Aberdeen, died in Oberwerth near Coblenz, Germany, on 2 July 1866. [DA.1625]

COBBAN, JAMES, son of James Cobban a merchant in Aberdeen, graduated MA from Marischal College in 1818, later a surgeon in Canada. [KCA][MCA]

COLLIE, ALEXANDER, a medical student in Aberdeen, was accused of violating sepulchres in 1812. [NRS.AD14.12.58]

COLLIE, DAVID, born 1800 in Aberdeen, died in St Ann's, Jamaica, on 6 March 1868. [AJ.15.4.1868]

COLLIE, GEORGE, son of George Collie a merchant in Aberdeen, was educated at Marischal College in 1841, later a merchant in Manchester. [MCA]

COLLIE, GEORGE, son of Robert Collie in Aberdeen, was educated at Marischal College in 1848, later an advocate in Aberdeen. [MCA]

COLLIE, JAMES, son of James Collie a woolcomber, was apprenticed to George Stott a weaver in Aberdeen from 1791 to 1796. [ACA]

COLLIE, JOHN, son of George Collie a merchant in Aberdeen, was educated at Marischal College in 1840. [MCA]

COLLIE, JOHN, a merchant in Aberdeen, father of James Mosses Collie, a merchant in the Seychelles, 1855. [NRS.S/H.1855]

COLLIE, WILLIAM, son of Alexander Collie in Aberdeen, was educated at Marischal College in 1842. [MCA]

COLLIE, WILLIAM, a bookseller, died in Chapel Street, Aberdeen, in 1846. [AJ.17.12.1846]

CONDELL, Mrs THOMAS H., from Aberdeen, died in Brooklyn, New York, in 1860. [AJ.31.10.1860]

CONDELL, ..., born 1788, a Major in Honourable East India Company Service, died in Aberdeen in 1853. [AJ.19.8.1853]

CONNAN, ALEXANDER, was admitted as a trade burgess of Old Aberdeen in October 1816. [ACA]

CONNAN, ALEXANDER, sr., was admitted as a tailor burgess of Old Aberdeen on 26 October 1818. [ACA]

CONNAN, ALEXANDER, jr., was admitted as a tailor burgess of Old Aberdeen on 16 October 1818. [ACA]

CONNAN, CHARLES W., from Old Machar, graduated MA from King's College, Aberdeen, in March 1834, later a schoolmaster in Liverpool. [KCA]

CONNAN, DAVID, was admitted as a merchant burgess of Old Aberdeen on 8 October 1808. [ACA]

CONNAN, DAVID, third son of James Connon, was admitted as a merchant burgess of Old Aberdeen on 18 February 1858. [ACA]

CONNAN, JAMES, was admitted as a trade burgess of Old Aberdeen in October 1816. [ACA]

CONNAN, JAMES, was admitted as a burgess of Old Aberdeen on 26 October 1818. [ACA]

CONNAN, ROBERT, eldest son of William Connon, was admitted as a burgess of Old Aberdeen on 31 October 1814. [ACA]

CONNAN, WILLIAM, was admitted as a merchant burgess of Old Aberdeen on 14 November 1799. [ACA]

COPLAND, CHARLES, from Aberdeen, died at Old Harbour, Jamaica, on 1 April 1820. [SM.86.95]

COOPER, ALEXANDER, born 1772, a manufacturer at Grandholm Works, died in 1838. [AJ.8.9.1838]

COOPER, JOHN, was admitted as a merchant burgess of Old Aberdeen on 30 October 1816. [ACA]

COOPER, JOHN, born 1797 in Aberdeen, took the Oath of Allegiance in Norfolk Borough Court, Virginia, on 26 December 1828. [NARA]

COOPER, JOHN, from Aberdeen, married Mary Hardwood Jennings, daughter of Joseph Jennings a merchant in Halifax, Nova Scotia, there on 1 April 1843. [NS:3.4.1843]

COOPER, WILLIAM, MD, born 1811, died in Aberdeen in 1838. [AJ.1.3.1838]

COPLAND, CHARLES, from Aberdeen, a cooper in Ostende, Flanders, in 1790. [NRS.S/H]

COPLAND, CHARLES, from Aberdeen, died at Old Harbour, Jamaica, on 6 April 1820. [BM.7.463]

COPLAND, JOHN, second son of Dr Copland, professor of Natural Philosophy in Marischal College, Aberdeen, of the Bombay Medical Establishment, India, died there in 1818. [AJ.12.12.1818]

COPLAND, MARY, only daughter of Dr Patrick Copland the Professor of Natural Philosophy at Marischal College, Aberdeen, married Alexander Murchison, MD of Jamaica, in Fountainhall, Aberdeen, on 8 October 1821. [BM.10.488]

COPLAND, PATRICK, born 1748, Professor of Natural Philosophy in Marischal College, Aberdeen, died in 1822. [AJ.10.11.1822]

COPLAND, WILLIAM, born 1750, elder of St Nicholas Church, Aberdeen, died in 1837. [AJ.24.11.1837]

CORBET, WILLIAM, born 1770, died in Aberdeen in 1841. [AJ.26.2.1841]

CORDINER, JAMES, born 1775, graduated MA from King's College, Aberdeen, in 1793, Episcopal minister of St Paul's Chapel, Aberdeen, from 1807 until 1834, died in 1836. [AJ.13.1.1836]

CORDINER, Mrs JANE MAXWELL, widow of Reverend James Cordiner of St Paul's Chapel, died at 108 Gallowgate, Aberdeen, in 1854. [AJ.14.8.1854]

CORVIE, ALEXANDER, born 1800, a labourer, with Janet Corvie, born 1806, Margaret Corvie, born 1828, George Corvie, born 1830, John Corvie, born 1831, Alexander Corvie, born 1834, James Corvie, born 1836, William Corvie, born 1839, and Janet Corvie, an infant, arrived in Kingston, Jamaica, on 11 May 1841 on board the Rob Roy from Aberdeen. [TNA.CO140/33]

COUTTS, ADAM, born 1777, an advocate, died at 65 Netherkirkgate, Aberdeen, in 1849. [AJ.11.4.1849]

COUTTS, JOHN, son of James Coutts a weaver, was apprenticed to William Leitch a coppersmith in Aberdeen from 1791 to 1796. [ACA]

COUTTS, WILLIAM, son of James Coutts a flaxdresser, was apprenticed to Peter Priest a cutler in Aberdeen, from 1788 to 1793. [ACA]

COWIE, ELIZABETH, born 1760, wife of Reverend Alexander Simpson, died at the Manse of New Machar, Aberdeen, in 1837. [AJ.8.1.1837]

COWIE, JOHN REID, in Indianapolis, Indiana, son and heir of Alexander Cowie a surgeon in Tanfield, Aberdeen, who died on 27 January 1851. [NRS.S/H]

COWIE, ROBERT, a wright from Aberdeen, later in New York, grandson and heir of William Watts a gardener in Aberdeen; also, to his mother Sarah Watts, widow of William Cowie a saddler in Aberdeen, who died on 28 March 1851. [NRS.S/H]

CRAIG, JOHN, son of Thomas Craig a merchant in Aberdeen, graduated MA from Marischal College in 1835, later a surgeon in the Service of the East India Company. [MCA]

CRANE, Captain, master of the Dove of Aberdeen from Fort William, with passengers bound for Pictou, Nova Scotia, in 1801. [NRS.RH2.4.87] [NLS.MS9646]

CRAN, ANDREW, born 1839, from Aberdeen, an overseer who died at Rose Hall, Berbice, on 21 September 1865. [AJ.25.10.1865]

CRIGHTON, JAMES, son of James Crighton a mariner in Aberdeen, was educated at Marischal College in 1841, later a minister. [MCA]

CROMAR, ALEXANDER, son of William Cromar in Aberdeen, was apprenticed to George Henderson, a weaver in Aberdeen, from 1791 to 1796, [ACA], was admitted as a weaver burgess of Old Aberdeen on 29 October 1821. [ACA]

CROMAR, ARTHUR, was admitted as a trade burgess of Old Aberdeen on 14 November 1817. [ACA]

CROMAR, JAMES, born 1765, Rector of Aberdeen Grammar School, died in Aberdeen in 1825. [AJ.10.11.1825]

CROMAR, WILLIAM, a gardener in Spital, son of David Cromar, was admitted as a weaver burgess of Old Aberdeen on 29 October 1859. [ACA]

CROMAR, Mrs, widow of James Cromar late Rector of Aberdeen Grammar School, died at 21 Silver Street, Aberdeen, in 1849. [AJ.13.8.1849]

CROMBIE, JAMES MORRISON, son of John Crighton a mariner in Aberdeen, was educated at Marischal College in 1847, later a minister. [MCA]

CRUDEN, Reverend ALEXANDER, formerly Rector of Farnham, Virginia, later settled in Aberdeen, probate 1792, PCC. [TNA]

CRUDEN, HELEN, born 1725, daughter of William Cruden a merchant and treasurer of Aberdeen, died in Aberdeen in 1808. [AJ.28.2.1808]

CRUICKSHANK, ALEXANDER, born 1798, a weaver in Aberdeen, was accused of 'southrief' in 1823. [NRS.AD14.23.216]

CRUICKSHANK, ALEXANDER, born 1827, from Aberdeen, died in Little Rock, Arkansas, in 1864. [AJ.16.11.1864]

CRUICKSHANK, ANDREW MICHAEL, born 16 September 1821 in Old Machar, son of William Cruickshank and his wife Mary Farquhar, late of Aberdeen, died in Woolcotville, Connecticut, on 14 December 1855. [AJ.16.1.1856]

CRUICKSHANK, BRODIE, from Aberdeen, graduated MA at King's College, Aberdeen, in 1841, later at Cape Coast Castle, West Africa. [KCA]

CRUICKSHANK, GEORGE, was admitted as a merchant burgess of Old Aberdeen on 5 October 1826. [ACA]

CRUICKSHANK, GEORGE, son of George Cruickshank, was admitted as a merchant burgess of Old Aberdeen on 26 October 1835. [ACA]

CRUICKSHANK, ISABELLA, born 1757, daughter of Robert Cruickshank, a baillie and merchant of Old Aberdeen, died in 1832. [AJ.12.10.1832]

CRUICKSHANK, JAMES, born 1829, son of Willian Cruickshank, [1789-1859], and his wife Jessie Fraser, [1804-1859], a printer who died in Memphis, Tennessee, on 8 September 1878. [St Peter's gravestone, Spittal, Aberdeen]

CRUICKSHANK, JAMES, son of William Cruickshank, a merchant in Aberdeen, was educated at Marischal College in 1844. [MCA]

CRUICKSHANK, JOHN, was educated at Marischal College, Aberdeen, in 1810, later a surgeon in St Helena. [MCA]

CRUICKSHANK, JOHN, jr. was admitted as a trade burgess of Old Aberdeen on 20 October 1820. [ACA]

CRUICKSHANK, JOHN, was admitted as a trade burgess of Old Aberdeen on 20 October 1820. [ACA]

CRUICKSHANK, LESLIE, born 1778, a merchant in Aberdeen, died in 1853. [AJ.1.2.1853]

CRUICKSHANK, MARGARET, widow of Samuel Hawkins Napier in Bathurst, New Brunswick, heir to Helen, widow of John Selbie a hosier in Aberdeen, 1865. [NRS.S/H]

CRUICKSHANK, MORRIS, son of John Cruickshank the minister of Glass, was educated at Marischal College in 1840s, later a surgeon with the East India Company. [MCA]

CRUICKSHANK, ROBERT, born 1748, probably from Aberdeen, a silversmith and merchant, settled in Montreal in 1773, died on 16 April 1809. [DCB]

CRUIKSHANK, WILLIAM, born in June 1760, son of Theodore Cruikshank and his wife Jane Allen in Bynsmill, Aberdeen, emigrated to Jamaica in 1781, later a carpenter in New York, married Sarah Allen in New York in 1795, died on 9 January 1831. [ANY]

CRUICKSHANK, WILLIAM, son of George Cruickshank in Aberdeen, was apprenticed to John Wallace a shoemaker in Aberdeen from 1786 to 1791. [ACA]

CUDDIE, ALEXANDER, MD, died at 31 Quay, Aberdeen, in 1851. [AJ.9.1.1852]

CUMINE, ADAM, born 1767, died at Albyn Place, Aberdeen, on 1841. [AJ.17.1.1841]

CUMINE, JOHN, was admitted as a brewer burgess of Old Aberdeen on 7 November 1801. [ACA]

CUMINE, JOHN, the younger of Auchry, died in Aberdeen in 1830. [AJ.1.2.1839]

CUMINE, MARGARET, born 1768, widow of Alexander Russell of Aden and Moncoffer, died in Aberdeen in 1841. [AJ.11.2.1841]

CUMMING, CATHERINE, born in Aberdeen, wife of James Lessel, died in Halifax, Nova Scotia, on 13 December 1858. [AJ.5.1.1859]

CUMMING, DAVID, a skipper in Aberdeen, his relict Katherine Marr, testament, 1821, Comm. Aberdeen. [NRS]

CUMMING, JANET, born 1815, with Mary Cumming, born 1817, arrived in Kingston, Jamaica, on 11 May 1841 on board the Rob Roy from Aberdeen. [TNA.CO140/33]

CUMMING, Captain, master of the Amity of Aberdeen from Aberdeen to the Bay of Chaleur, New Brunswick in 1839. [AJ]

CUSHNIE, JOHN, born 1728, a shipmaster, died in Aberdeen in 1801. [AJ.4.5.1801]

CUSHNIE, WILLIAM, a mariner in Aberdeen, testament, 1822, Comm. Edinburgh. [NRS]

DALGARNO, ALEXANDER, son of James Dalgarno, a merchant in Aberdeen, was educated at Marischal College in 1848, died as a student. [MCA]

DALGARNO, WILLIAM, was admitted as a tailor burgess of Old Aberdeen on 29 October 1832. [ACA]

DALGARNO, Mrs, daughter of John Skinner senior bishop and Primus of the Scottish Episcopal Church, and widow of Alexander Dalgarno, a merchant in Aberdeen, died at 7 Union Terrace, Aberdeen, in 1850. [AJ.7.1.1851]

DANIEL, JAMES, born 1825, Sheriff Clerk Depute of Aberdeen, died in 1848. [AJ.4.13.1848]

DANIEL, JAMES, son of John Daniel, was admitted as a burgess of Old Aberdeen on 25 November 1854. [ACA]

DANIEL, JOHN, was admitted as a trade burgess of Old Aberdeen on 18 January 1819. [ACA]

DANIEL, WILLIAM, son of Thomas Daniel, an innkeeper in Aberdeen, later Sheriff Clerk Depute of Aberdeen. [MCA]

DANIEL, Captain, master of the Lion of Aberdeen from Aberdeen to Quebec in 1858. [AJ]

DAUNEY, Dr ALEXANDER, born 1749, Professor of Civil Law at King's College, Aberdeen, died there in 1833. [AJ.14.7.1833]

DAVIDSON, ANDREW, a surgeon from Aberdeen, died on Curriacou near Grenada, on 3 November 1802. [EA]

DAVIDSON, ANNIE, in Appleton City, Missouri, heir to her grandfather John Davidson a merchant in Aberdeen, who died 2 December 1853. [NRS.S/H]

DAVIDSON, CATHERINE, daughter of Dr Davidson in Rayne, Aberdeenshire, died in Aberdeen in 1828. [AJ.28.7.1828]

DAVIDSON, CHARLES, born 1806, a house servant in Aberdeen, was accused of assault in Turriff, Aberdeenshire, in 1835. [NRS.AD14.35.70]

DAVIDSON, DUNCAN, an advocate in Aberdeen, witnessed a deed in Aberdeen on 7 March 1807. [NRS.RD5.271.168]

DAVIDSON, GEORGE, son of James Davidson a merchant in Aberdeen, a student at Marischal College in the 1790s. [MCA]

DAVIDSON, GORDON FORBES, born 1807, son of Andrew Davidson an advocate in Aberdeen, and his wife Barbara Forbes, a student at Marischal College in 1820s, died in New South Wales, Australia, on 17 October 1865. [St Nicholas gravestone, Aberdeen] [MCA]

DAVIDSON, HENRY SHIRLEY, son of John Davidson in Kingston, Jamaica, died in Aberdeen on 31 October 1799. [EA.3746.334]

DAVIDSON, JAMES, formerly a thread manufacturer in Aberdeen, died at Springhill, Galt, Canada, in 1852. [AJ.15.8.1852]

DAVIDSON, JOHN, born 1792, son of Andrew Davidson an advocate in Aberdeen, and his wife Barbara Forbes, died in Java, Dutch East Indies, in 1841. [St Nicholas gravestone, Aberdeen]

DAVIDSON, JOHN, a weaver in College Street, Aberdeen, was accused of housebreaking and theft in 1817. [NRS.AC17.14.40]

DAVIDSON, JOHN, of Kebbaty, born 1750, died in Aberdeen in 1824. [AJ.7.1.1824]

DAVIDSON, JOHN, born 1805, a shoemaker at Bridge of Don, Old Machar, Aberdeen, was accused of assault in 1824. [NRS.AD14.24.126]

DAVIDSON, JOHN, a writer in Aberdeen, nephew and heir of John Blyth a planter in Jamaica, 1849. [NRS.S/H]

DAVIDSON, JOHN, a merchant in Aberdeen, died 2 December 1853, grandfather of Annie Davidson and of Nancy Woodburn in Appleton, Missouri, by 1890. [NRS.S/H]

DAVIDSON, JONATHAN, born 1797, son of Andrew Davidson an advocate in Aberdeen, and his wife Barbara Forbes, graduated MA from Marischal College in 1813, died in Mauritius in 1854. [St Nicholas gravestone, Aberdeen] [MCA]

DAVIDSON, PETER, a skipper in Aberdeen, his relict Margaret Taylor in Rathes, testament, Comm. Aberdeen, 1815. [NRS]

DAVIDSON, PETER, born 1802, only son of Peter Davidson in Aberdeen, fell from the foreyard of the Waterloo to his death on 15 March 1823 in St John, New Brunswick. [CG.20.3.1823]

DAVIDSON, RICHARD RICH MILFORD, born 1809, son of Andrew Davidson an advocate in Aberdeen, and his wife Barbara Forbes, died in Singapore in 1831. [St Nicholas gravestone, Aberdeen]

DAVIDSON, WILLIAM, was admitted as a trade burgess of Old Aberdeen in October 1816. [ACA]

DAVIDSON, WILLIAM, a shoemaker in Aberdeen, was accused of housebreaking and theft in 1817. [NRS.AC17.14.40]

DAVIDSON, WILLIAM, was admitted as a cartwright burgess of Old Aberdeen on 19 December 1856. [ACA]

DAVIDSON, Mrs, of Kebbaty, born 1810, died at 91 Broad Street, Aberdeen, in 1844. [AJ.11.3.1844]

DAVNIE, ELIZABETH JANET, from Aberdeen, married James Law, a merchant in Auburn, in New York on 24 July 1838. [AJ.4730] [MacGregor's Gazette.1.12]

DAWSON, JOHN, a merchant from Aberdeen, died in Demerara on 17 February 1857. [AJ.17.6.1857]

DEANS, WILLIAM, was admitted as a weaver burgess of Old Aberdeen on 26 October 1801. [ACA]

DEMPSTER, Captain JOHN, master of the Amity of Aberdeen with passengers from Aberdeen bound for Dalhousie, New Brunswick in 1840. [AJ]

DESSON, WILLIAM, born 1818, a millwright, with Ann Desson, born 1819, arrived in Kingston, Jamaica, on 11 May 1841 on board the Rob Roy from Aberdeen. [TNA.CO140/33]

DEVINE, FRANCIS, born 1806, a labourer, with Ann Devine, born 1808, John Devine, born 1832, Ann Devine, born 1833, Mary Devine, born 1835, Francis Devine, born 1837, and Margaret Devine, born 1840, arrived in Kingston, Jamaica, on 11 May 1841 on board the Rob Roy from Aberdeen. [TNA.CO140/33]

DEVINE, JAMES, from Aberdeen, graduated MA from King's College, Aberdeen, in March 1840, later an Episcopalian minister in Canada. [KCA]

DICKIE, JOHN, emigrated from Aberdeen aboard the Albion of Aberdeen bound for Halifax, Nova Scotia, in 1836. [AJ.29.6.1836]

DINGWALL, ALEXANDER, jr., postmaster, died at Springbank, Aberdeen, in 1834. [AJ.3.3.1834]

DOIG, Reverend ROBERT, born 1768, minister of St Nicholas, Aberdeen, died in Edinburgh in 1824. [AJ.26.7.1824]

DONALD, JOHN, born 1839, a paper ruler, son of George Donald, [1799-1849], a mason in Aberdeen, died in the West Indies on 7 May 1860. [St Peter's gravestone, Spittal, Aberdeen]

DONALD, WILLIAM, from Aberdeen, graduated MA from King's College in 1832, later a schoolmaster in Huntly, then a minister in St John, New Brunswick. [KCA]

DONALDSON, CHARLES, an Advocate and Procurator Fiscal of the Peace for Aberdeenshire, died in Aberdeen in 1824. [AJ.16.4.1824] [BM.22.768]

DONALDSON, WILLIAM, born 1838, son of Alexander Donaldson a butcher in Aberdeen, died in New York aboard the Edwin Forrest on 6 April 1854. [AJ.7.6.1854]

DOW, ALEXANDER, a meat seller in Aberdeen, was accused of bigamy in 1817. [NRS.AD14.17.145]

DOWELL, JOHN, son of Robert Dowell, a merchant in Aberdeen, was educated at Marischal College in 1844. [MCA]

DOWER, JANE, in Millbank, Canada West, sister and heir of Helen Dower, widow of James Mortimer in Aberdeen, who died 17 November 1866. [NRS.S/H]

DOWNIE, JOHN, a farmer at Standing Stones, Old Machar, brother and heir of Andrew Downie in Ohio, who died on 13 May 1844. [NRS.S/H]

DUFF, ALEXANDER, born 1799 in Aberdeen, eldest son of Archibald Duff a Professor of Dancing, an organist and Professor of Music, died in Montreal, Quebec, on 7 December 1838. [AJ.4750]

DUFF, ARCHIBALD, son of Archibald Duff a magistrate in Aberdeen, a student at Marischal College in 1820s, later a minister in Canada, graduated DD from Vermont University. [MCA]

DUFF, JOHN, born 1812, a carpenter, arrived in Kingston, Jamaica, on 11 May 1841 on board the Rob Roy from Aberdeen. [TNA.CO140/33]

DUGUID, JOHN, born 1779, Captain of the Aberdeen Militia, Dee Street, Aberdeen, was accused of murder by duelling in 1824. [NRS.AD14.24.389]

DUGUID, MARY ANN, wife of James Malcolm in Hamilton, Canada West, heir to her grandmother Janet Aiken, widow of W. Duguid a manufacturer in Aberdeen, who died on 3 October 1862. [NRS.S/H]

DUGUID, PETER, born 1747, a baillie, died in Aberdeen in 1809. [AJ.13.7.1809]

DUGUID, THOMAS, son of Patrick Duguid a merchant in Aberdeen, was educated at Marischal College in 1814, later a merchant in Liverpool and in Buenos Ayres, Argentina. [MCA]

DUGUID, WILLIAM, born 1757, a merchant in Aberdeen, died in 1805. [AJ.20.2.1805]

DUNBAR, DUNCAN, was admitted as a trade burgess of Old Aberdeen on 30 October 1820. [ACA]

DUNBAR, PETER, son of William Dunbar, was admitted as a trade burgess of Old Aberdeen on 24 April 1815. [ACA]

DUNBAR, WILLIAM, was admitted as a merchant burgess of Old Aberdeen on 24 April 1815. [ACA]

DUNCAN, ADAM, a merchant, married Caroline Elliot, eldest daughter of Thomas Elliot, from Heathfield, America, in Aberdeen, on 4 December 1823. [DPCA.1116]

DUNCAN, ADAM, an assistant surgeon of the 67th Regiment, died in St Joseph's, Trinidad, on 7 October 1838. [AJ.4745]

DUNCAN, ALEXANDER, in Tobago, father of Alexander Duncan a student at Marischal College, Aberdeen, in 1790s. [MCA]

DUNCAN, ALEXANDER, son of Alexander Duncan in Aberdeen, graduated MA from Marischal College in 1819, later a surgeon in the Service of the East India Company. [MCA]

DUNCAN, Captain ALEXANDER, sr., a skipper in Aberdeen, testament, 1819, Comm. Aberdeen. [NRS]

DUNCAN, ALEXANDER, jr., a skipper in Aberdeen, testament, 1819, Comm. Aberdeen. [NRS]

DUNCAN, ALEXANDER, was admitted as a trade burgess of Old Aberdeen In April 1820. [ACA]

DUNCAN, ALEXANDER, master of the Carolina of Aberdeen with passengers from Aberdeen to Quebec in 1815. [NRS.E501.25]

DUNCAN, ALEXANDER SHUTER, son of Alexander Duncan, a merchant in Aberdeen, was at Marischal College in 1840. [MCA]

DUNCAN, ALEXANDER, born 1809, a labourer, with Isabella Duncan, born 1811, Jane Duncan, born 1833, William Duncan, born 1835, Margaret Duncan, born 1837, and Isabella Duncan, born 1840, arrived in Kingston, Jamaica, on 11 May 1841 on board the Rob Roy from Aberdeen. [TNA.CO140/33]

DUNCAN, CHARLES, son of William Duncan, a merchant in Aberdeen, was educated at Marischal College in 1846. [MCA]

DUNCAN, CHARLES, son of William Duncan, a mariner in Aberdeen, was educated at Marischal College in 1844, later an advocate in Aberdeen. [MCA]

DUNCAN, ISABEL, sometime spouse to Chevalier Tournier or French, late tobacconist in Aberdeen, later spouse to John Hill at Aberdeen Green, testament, 17 January 1798, Comm. Aberdeen. [NRS]

DUNCAN, JAMES, a skipper in Aberdeen, son of James Duncan a baker in Aberdeen, testament, 1820, Comm. Aberdeen. [NRS]

DUNCAN, JAMES, in Renny's Wynd, Aberdeen, victim of assault in 1824. [NRS.AD14.24.126]

DUNCAN, JOHN, of Mostown, a merchant and sometime Provost of Aberdeen, testament, 7 November 1799, Comm. Aberdeen. [NRS]

DUNCAN, JOHN, a mariner in Aberdeen, testament, 1808, Comm. Aberdeen. [NRS]

DUNCAN, JOHN, emigrated from Aberdeen on board the Albion of Aberdeen bound for Halifax, Nova Scotia, in 1836. [AJ.29.6.1836]

DUNCAN, JOHN, son of John Duncan, a shoemaker in Aberdeen, was educated at Marischal College in 1848. [MCA]

DUNCAN, JOHN, son of William Duncan, a mariner in Aberdeen, was educated at Marischal College in 1844, later a Canon of Salisbury Cathedral. [MCA]

DUNCAN, JOHN, born 1814, a carpenter, arrived in Kingston, Jamaica, on 11 May 1841 on board the Rob Roy from Aberdeen. [TNA.CO140/33]

DUNCAN, ROBERT B., son of William Duncan a schoolmaster in Aberdeen, graduated MA from Marischal College in 1818, later a surgeon in the Service of the East India Company. [MC]

DUNCAN, WILLIAM, was admitted as a trade burgess of Old Aberdeen on 8 October 1808. [ACA]

DUNCAN, WILLIAM, son of William Duncan, a supervisor in Aberdeen, was educated at Marischal College in 1849. [MCA]

DUNCAN, WILLIAM, son of George Duncan, a stonemason in Aberdeen, was educated at Marischal College in 1840. [MCA]

DUNN, JAMES, born 1804, master of Aberdeen Grammar School, died in 1847. [AJ.18.12.1847]

DUNN, JOHN, was admitted as a trade burgess of Old Aberdeen on 18 January 1819. [ACA]

DUNN, JOHN, son of Joseph Dunn, was admitted as a trade burgess of Old Aberdeen on 24 October 1857. [ACA]

DUNN, JOSEPH, was admitted as a brewer burgess of Old Aberdeen on 25 October 1851. [ACA]

DUNN, WILLIAM, son of John Dunn, a merchant in Aberdeen, was educated at Marischal College in 1843, later an advocate in Aberdeen. [MCA]

DUNSMURE, JOHN, born 1840 in Aberdeen, a carpenter on the City of Glasgow, died in Demerara on 24 November 1866. [AJ.16.1.1867]

DURNO, GEORGE, a brassfounder from Aberdeen, died in Tremont, Westchester County, New York, on 12 March 1865. [AJ.5.4.1865]

DURNO, Mrs JANE, born 1803, wife of James Durno, late of Aberdeen, died in Upper Alton, Illinois, on 21 August 1841. [AJ.4900]

DURNO, JOHN, an advocate from Aberdeen, died in Jamaica in 1817. [S.6.17]

DUTHIE, ALEXANDER, son of William Duthie a merchant in Aberdeen, graduated MA from Marischal College, Aberdeen, in 1794. [MCA]

DUTHIE, CHARLES, son of William Duthie in Aberdeen, was educated at Marischal College in 1840. [MCA]

DUTHIE, or LAWRENCE, or LEE, HELEN, wife of R. H. Lee a merchant in Buffalo, New York, heir of William Duthie a merchant in Aberdeen, 1847; also, to Helen Milne, wife of William Duthie a mason in Aberdeen, 1847. [NRS.S/H]

DUTHIE, WILLIAM, son of John Duthie a tailor, was apprenticed to John Webster, a weaver in Aberdeen, from 1789 to 1794. [ACA]

DUTHIE, Captain, master of the City of Aberdeen from Aberdeen with passengers bound for Quebec in 1826. [Canadian Courier and Montreal Advertiser]

DYCE, ALEXANDER, a merchant in Aberdeen, testament, 3 April 1797, Comm. Aberdeen. [NRS]

DYCE, HELEN OGILVIE, daughter of James Dyce in Aberdeen, married Reverend James Soutar, a pastor in Newcastle, New Brunswick, in Halifax, Nova Scotia, on 1 September 1831. [AR.3.9.1831]

DYCE, JANET, born 1722, widow of William Forbes a coppersmith in Aberdeen, died there in 1803. [AJ.25.11.1803]

DYCE, KATHERINE, relict of Alexander Finnie, in Aberdeen, testament, 4 December 1792, Comm. Aberdeen. [NRS]

DYCE, LOWRY WILLIAM FREDERICK, son of Robert Dyce MD, was educated at Marischal College in 1846. [MCA]

EDMOND, ALEXANDER, from Aberdeen, a merchant in St John, New Brunswick, died in Edinburgh on 5 April 1825 when bound for his birthplace, testament, 1825, Comm. Edinburgh. [NRS] [NBC.21 5.1825]

EDMOND, JAMES, son of James Edmond an advocate in Aberdeen, a student at Marischal College in 1850s, later in Canada. [MCA]

EDMOND, JOHN, was admitted as a trade burgess of Old Aberdeen on 17 March 1807. [ACA]

EDWARDS, J., born in Aberdeen, married Miss E. M. Wood in Sydney, New South Wales, Australia, on 12 March 1862. [AJ.5968]

ELLIOT, J., master of the Berbice of Aberdeen from Aberdeen with passengers bound for Quebec in 1848, 1852, 1853, and 1854. [AJ]

ELMSLIE, JAMES, was admitted as a cooper burgess of Old Aberdeen on 1 October 1810. [ACA]

ELMSLIE, JOHN, son of Alexander Elmslie, was apprenticed to William Strachan, a baker in Aberdeen, from 1794 to 1799. [ACA]

ELMSLEY, JOSEPH, emigrated from Aberdeen on board the Albion of Aberdeen bound for Halifax, Nova Scotia, in 1836. [AJ.29.6.1836]

ELMSLY, THOMAS, born 1819, third son of Mr Elmsly of Pitmeddan, died in Aberdeen in 1849. [AJ.18.9.1849]

ELMSLIE, WILLIAM, from Aberdeen, was educated at King's College, Aberdeen, in 1857, a physician in India. [KCA.308]

ELPHINSTON, Mrs JANET, relict of Dr George Chalmers a physician in Aberdeen, testament, 16 February 1792, Comm. Aberdeen. [NRS]

ENGLAND, JOHN, was admitted as a tailor burgess of Old Aberdeen on 30 October 1809. [ACA]

ENGLISH, WILLIAM, master of the Nautilius of Aberdeen from Aberdeen with passengers bound for Newfoundland, Cape Breton, and Barbados in 1835. [AJ.4551]

EWEN, JOHN, born 1769, a wood merchant in Aberdeen, died at Ewen Place, Aberdeen, in 1849. [AJ.29.7.1849]

FAIRBAIRN, Mrs DOROTHY, of Hopewell, residing in Aberdeen, testament, 24 November 1792, Comm. Aberdeen. [NRS]

FALCONER, DANIEL, born 1816, a millwright, arrived in Kingston, Jamaica, on 11 May 1841 on board the Rob Roy from Aberdeen. [TNA.CO140/33]

FALCONER, JAMES, a purser of the Royal Navy, sometime in Stonehaven, later in the Hardgate of Aberdeen, testament, 17 November 1791, Comm. Aberdeen. [NRS]

FALCONER, JAMES, was admitted as a tanner burgess of Old Aberdeen on 31 October 1795. [ACA]

FARQUHAR, ISABEL, housekeeper in Aberdeen Infirmary, testament, 22 April 1795, Comm. Aberdeen. [NRS]

FARQUHAR, JAMES, a surgeon in the Royal Navy, testament, 1819, Comm. Aberdeen. [NRS]

FARQUHAR, JOHN, in Jamaica, heir to James Farquhar a land surveyor in Aberdeen in 1806. [NRS.S/H]

FARQUHAR, NATHANIEL, an advocate in Aberdeen, died on 19 July 1861, father of Allan Farquhar in Ban Ban, Queensland, Australia. [NRS.S/H]

FARQUHAR, ROBERT, son of John and Elizabeth Farquhar in Aberdeen, a merchant in Charleston, South Carolina, was naturalised there on 24 January 1783, probate 17 February 1784, S.C.

FARQUHARSON, CHARLES, born 1753, a merchant and magistrate of Aberdeen, died in 1809. [AJ.6.12.1809]

FARQUHARSON, GEORGE CAMPBELL, eldest son of P. Farquharson of Whitehouse, died at 15 Union Terrace, Aberdeen, in 1838. [AJ.8.9.1838]

FARQUHARSON, JOHN or JAMES [?], a physician in Charleston, South Carolina, a Loyalist who moved to London by 1780, died in Old Aberdeen on 18 October 1790, probate January 1791, PCC. [TNA][GM.60.1053] [TNA.AO12.47.415]

FARQUHARSON, MARGARET, born 1761, daughter of Alexander Farquharson of Inverey, died in Aberdeen in 1826. [AJ.16.5.1826]

FENWICK, Captain, master of the <u>Bolivar of Aberdeen</u> from the River Clyde to Quebec in 1832. [GA.3417]

FERGUSON, ANDREW, MD, born 1813, son of Andrew Ferguson in Aberdeen, died in Kingston, Jamaica, on 30 August 1853. [AJ.5.10.1853]

FERGUSON, ELIZA, born 1806, eldest daughter of Andrew Ferguson a physician in Aberdeen, died in 1824. [AJ.9.1.1825]

FERGUSON, GEORGE, a mariner in Aberdeen, testament, 1821, Comm. Aberdeen. [NRS]

FERGUSON, JAMES, eldest son of James Ferguson a merchant in Aberdeen, died in Halifax, Nova Scotia, in 1817. [S.41.17]

FERGUSON, JAMES, in Aberdeen, applied to settle in Canada on 3 April 1827. [TNA.CO384.5.843]

FERGUSON, JAMES, MA, son of Andrew Ferguson a surgeon in Aberdeen, was educated at King's College, Aberdeen, from 1816 to 1820, Rector of Rutgers College, New Jersey, and Superintendent of Public Schools in Lockport, New York. [KCA]

FERGUSON, ROBERT, in Aberdeen, was admitted as a dyer burgess of Old Aberdeen on 30 October 1843. [ACA]

FERGUSON, WILLIAM, baptised on 27 May 1803 in St Nicholas, Aberdeen, son of John Ferguson and his wife Sarah Mearns, was educated at Marischal College, Aberdeen, from 1817 to 1821, a catechist in Canada, later an Inspector of Schools in Dundas County, Ontario. [F.1.633] [KCA]

FERNIE, JAMES, was admitted as a trade burgess of Old Aberdeen on 30 October 1820. [ACA]

FERRIER, CHARLES, and his wife Isabel Greg in Aberdeen, parents of Alexander born on 22 November 1850, educated at Aberdeen University in 1877, a chaplain in India from 1878 to 1900. [F.7.572]

FERRIER, JOHN, ships carpenter in Aberdeen, formerly in Banff, testament, 28 April 1794, Comm. Aberdeen. [NRS]

FERRIS, JOHN, born 1804 in Aberdeen, with his wife Janet, born 1806 in Aberdeen, and daughter Ellen born 1828, settled by the Swan River, Australia, by 1830. [BPP]

FERRIS, ROBERT, born 1810 in Aberdeen, a servant, settled by the Swan River, Australia, by 1830. [BPP]

FETTES, JAMES, son of Alexander Fettes a cartwright in Old Aberdeen, was apprenticed to Margaret Morice a baker in Aberdeen from 1792 to 1797. [ACA]

FETTES, JOHN, son of William Fettes a salmon fisher at Bridge of Don, was apprenticed to John Wallace a baker in Aberdeen from 1788 to 1793. [ACA]

FETTES, RICHARD, was admitted as a butcher burgess of Old Aberdeen on 17 November 1810. [ACA]

FETTES, WILLIAM, at Bridge of Don, was admitted as a butcher burgess of Old Aberdeen on 10 November 1792. [ACA]

FIDDES, ALEXANDER, son of George Fiddes, was admitted as a burgess of Old Aberdeen in April 1812. [ACA]

FIDDES, GEORGE, son of George Fiddes, was admitted as a burgess of Old Aberdeen on 14 November 1799. [ACA]

FIDDES, GEORGE, son of Alexander Fiddes, was admitted as a painter burgess of Old Aberdeen on 14 November 1835. [ACA]

FIDDES, PETER, was admitted as a merchant burgess of Old Aberdeen on 8 October 1808. [ACA]

FIDDES, ROBERT, son of Peter Fiddes, was admitted as a merchant burgess of Old Aberdeen on 28 October 1822. [ACA]

FINDLAY, THOMAS, son of James Findlay, [1780-1852], and his wife Barbara Marshall, [1794-868], died in New Orleans in 1840. [St Clement's gravestone, Aberdeen]

FINDLAY, WILLIAM, born 1797, a ploughman, arrived in Kingston, Jamaica, on 11 May 1841 on board the Rob Roy from Aberdeen. [TNA.CO140/33]

FINDLAY, Captain, master of the Alexander Hall of Aberdeen, from Aberdeen with passengers bound for Quebec in 1854. [AH]

FINLAYSON, ALEXANDER, born 1817 in Aberdeen, settled in Charleston, South Carolina, in 1836, died there on 14 October 1851. [AJ]

FINLAYSON, JOHN, jr., was admitted as a tailor burgess of Old Aberdeen on 29 October 1832. [ACA]

FINLAYSON, MARY ALLEN, daughter of William Allen in Mile-end, Aberdeen, died in Fredericksburg, Demerara, on 22 January 1866. [AJ.14.3.1866]

FINNIE, KATHERINE, in Aberdeen, testament, 3 June 1791, Comm. Aberdeen. [NRS]

FLEMING, ANDREW, from Old Machar, graduated MA from King's College, Aberdeen, in March 1838, later a surgeon in the Service of the East India Company. [KCA]

FLEMING, GEORGE, son of James Fleming a mason in Aberdeen, was apprenticed to Garvock and White, staymakers in Aberdeen, from 1785 to 1792. [ACA]

FLEMING, JAMES, son of ……. Fleming and his wife Grace Robertson, [1776-1850], a seedsman in Toronto. [St Clement's gravestone, Aberdeen]

FLEMING, JOHN, born in Aberdeen, settled in Canada in 1804, President of the Bank of Montreal, died on 30 September 1832. [AJ.4422]

FLEMING, or LORIMER, ROBERT, born 1806, a linen weaver in Gallowgate, Aberdeen, was accused of theft in 1820. [NRS.AD14.20.261]

FORBES, ALEXANDER, a merchant in Aberdeen, testament, 22 March 1797, Comm. Aberdeen. [NRS]

FORBES, ALEXANDER, a wine merchant in Aberdeen, and his wife Janet, parents of Duncan Forbes, a merchant in Amoy, China. [NRS.S/H]

FORBES, ANN, third daughter of James Forbes in Kingsland Place, Aberdeen, married Reverend Alexander Gardiner of Fergus, Upper Canada, in Quebec on 16 August 1838. [AJ.4731]

FORBES, ARTHUR, a Lieutenant Colonel, born 1760, youngest son of Sir Arthur Forbes of Craigievar, died in Old Aberdeen in 1850. [AJ.10.12.1850]

FORBES, Reverend FRANCIS, born on 27 September 1804 in Old Machar, Aberdeen, son of Dr Patrick Forbes of King's College, graduated MA from King's College in 1821, minister of St Luke's in Demerara, died on 8 December 1855. [KCA][AJ.5636] [F.7.677]

FORBES, GEORGE, a coppersmith and a magistrate of Aberdeen, testament, 9 May 1793, Comm. Aberdeen. [NRS]

FORBES, GEORGE, son of George Forbes in Gallowgate, Aberdeen, died in Grenada on 15 May 1802. [SM.64.616]

FORBES, JAMES, son of George Forbes a tailor burgess, was apprenticed to James Clerk a factor and tailor in Aberdeen, from 1787 to 1792. [ACA]

FORBES, JAMES, youngest son of Dr James Forbes a physician in Aberdeen, a merchant in New York who died at sea on passage from Savannah, Georgia, on 26 September 1819. [

FORBES, Dr JAMES, born in Aberdeen, the Inspector General of Army Hospitals, died in London in 1837. [AJ.7.11.1837]

FORBES, JAMES STAATS, born 1765, died in Aberdeen in 1845. [AJ.4.7.1845]

FORBES, JAMES MOIR, editor of the 'Aberdeen Journal', married Sarah James Robertson, third daughter of George Robertson in Aberdeen, in Quebec on 23 October 1838. [AJ.4744]

FORBES, JAMES, [1824-1865], and his wife Ann McDonald, [1822-1916], parents of John Forbes, born 1864, died in Delaware in 1903. [St Clement's gravestone, Aberdeen]

FORBES, JANET, widow of James Allardyce 'for many years Collector of HM Customs, died in Aberdeen in 1829. [AJ.13.6.1829]

FORBES, JOHN, born 6 March 1788 in Aberdeen, son of John Forbes of Blackford and his wife Margaret Gregory, a cadet in the Bengal Army, died at sea on 5 February 1805. [BA.2.201]

FORBES, JOHN, from Aberdeen, married Ann Kidd, in Montreal, on 21 August 1833. [AJ.4464]

FORBES, KATHERINE ANN BUCHAN, born 1810, daughter of Major Alexander Forbes of Invernernan, and wife of William McCombie of Easter Skene, died in Aberdeen in 1835. [AJ.16.4.1835]

FORBES, MARGARET, daughter of Reverend William Forbes of Fordoun, and grand-daughter of Thomas Forbes of Thornton, died in Aberdeen in 1833. [AJ.7.12.1833]

FORBES, Mrs MARY, born 1785, daughter of Reverend Duff of Foveran, and wife of Alexander Forbes in Jamaica, died in Aberdeen in 1808. [AJ.13.2.1808]

FORBES, Reverend PATRICK, DD, minister of Old Machar, Aberdeen, and Professor of Humanity in King's College, Aberdeen, died in 1847. [AJ.13.10.1847]

FORBES, PETER, was admitted as a trade burgess of Old Aberdeen on 31 October 1814. [ACA]

FORBES, THOMAS, a shipmaster in Aberdeen, husband of Catherine Syme testament, 1794, Comm. Edinburgh. [NRS]

FORBES, WILLIAM, in Jamaica, heir to his mother Jean Lumsden, wife of George Forbes a merchant in Aberdeen, in 1814. [NRS.S/H]

FORBES, WILLIAM, son of Alexander Forbes a merchant in Aberdeen, was educated at Marischal College around 1836, later a Major General of the Bengal Army. [MCA]

FORDYCE, ALEXANDER DINGWALL, son of Alexander Fordyce a merchant in Aberdeen, was educated at Marischal College in 1830s, died in Fergus, Canada West, in 1852. [MCA][AJ.23.2.1852]

FORDYCE, ANDREW WATSON, of Ardoe, born 1811, died in Aberdeen in 1837. [AJ.4.4.1837]

FORDYCE, WILLIAM DINGWALL, of Techmuiry, a writer in Aberdeen, born 1776, son of Arthur Dingwall Fordyce the commissary of Aberdeenshire, was admitted as a Notary Public on 17 January 1794, died in Aberdeen on 1 March 1831. [NRS.NP2.35.103] [AJ.1.3.1831]

FORDYCE, WILLIAM DINGWALL, born 22 September 1798, second son of William Dingwall Fordyce and his wife Margaret Ritchie, a merchant who died in Charleston, South Carolina, on 13 April 1839. [Society of Advocates in Aberdeen]

FORSYTH, ALEXANDER, was educated at Marischal College in 1815, graduated MA from King's College, Aberdeen, in 1817, settled in Halifax, Nova Scotia. [MCA]

FORSYTH, HELEN, eldest daughter of James Forsyth a baker from Aberdeen, married Walter Sloan from Penn County, Pennsylvania, at Mac's Hotel on the Ovens River on 29 July 1862. [AJ.5990]

FORSYTH, Reverend Dr JAMES, and his wife Elizabeth Brown who died 28 January 1854, parents of James Forsyth a Lieutenant of the Indian Army. [NRS.S/H.1863], and of John Smith Forsyth, born 1 January 1840 in Aberdeen, who died in Melbourne, Australia, on 20 November 1885. [F.6.40]

FORSYTH, JOHN, a leather merchant in Aberdeen, father of George Michie Forsyth, born 1851, died aboard the Collingrove bound for Adelaide, South Australia, on 8 December 1875. [AJ.6686]

FOULARTON, ROBERT, son of Alexander Foularton in Aberdeen, was educated at King's College, Aberdeen in 1818, settled in Chicago, Illinois. [KCA.2.432]

FRASER, ALEXANDER, son of Alexander Fraser a merchant in Aberdeen, graduated MA from Marischal College in 1833, later a merchant in Java, Dutch East Indies. [MCA]

FRASER, ANN, born 1778, spouse of John Duffus and engineer in Footdee, Aberdeen, died in 1831. [AJ.26.4.1831]

FRASER, Reverend CHARLES, born 1788, a Roman Catholic clergyman, died in Aberdeen in 1835. [AJ.12.3.1835]

FRASER, CHARLES, son of Hugh Fraser a merchant in Aberdeen, graduated MA from Marischal College in 1842, later a Free Church minister in New Zealand. [MCA]

FRASER, FORBES, born 1817, a blacksmith, with Ann Fraser, born 1817, arrived in Kingston, Jamaica, on 11 May 1841 on board the Rob Roy from Aberdeen. [TNA.CO140/33]

FRASER, GEORGE, a joiner from Aberdeen, died in New Orleans, Louisiana, on 31 August 1867. [AJ.23.10.1867]

FRASER, ISAAC, a vintner in Aberdeen, testament, 2 August 1800, Comm. Aberdeen. [NRS]

FRASER, JAMES, master of the Economy of Aberdeen from Tobermory with passengers to Pictou, Nova Scotia, in 1819. [AR.16.10.1819]

FRASER, JOHN, born 1778 in Aberdeen, died in Halifax, Nova Scotia, on 7 May 1831. [AR.14.5.1831]

FRASER, MARGARET, born 1827 in Aberdeen, died at Montego Bay, Jamaica, in 1852. [AJ.16.6.1852]

FRASER, SIMON, was educated at King's College, Aberdeen, graduated MA in 1835, later a minister in MacNab, Canada. [KCA]

FRASER, WILLIAM, son of Alexander Fraser an advocate in Aberdeen, was educated at Marischal College in 1859, later was the Superintendent of Police in Natal, South Africa. [MCA]

FRATER, ALEXANDER, son of James Frater a clerk in Aberdeen, graduated MA from Marischal College in 1848, later the British Consul in China. [MCA]

FRATER, JAMES, and his wife Mary Lowe in Aberdeen, parents of Arthur Wellesley Frater, born 20 October 1852, was educated at Aberdeen University in1875, a minister in Zealand and Flanders from 1884. [F.7.549]

FRENCH, EDWARD, son of Edward French a weaver, was apprenticed to Alexander Paterson, a shoemaker in Aberdeen, from 1785 to 1790. [ACA]

FRENCH, Dr GEORGE, born 1751, a physician in Aberdeen and Professor of Chemistry in Marischal College, died in 1833. [AJ.13.8.1833]

FYFE, JAMES, was admitted as a butcher burgess of 1850. [C] Aberdeen on 24 October 1857. [ACA]

FYFE, JOHN, a surgeon in the Royal Navy, later in Aberdeen, testament, 1794, Comm. Aberdeen. [NRS]

FYVIE, WILLIAM, born 1790 in Aberdeen, a Congregationalist minister, settled in Tisbury, Duke's County, Massachusetts by 1850. [C]

GAIR, JOHN, was admitted as a trade burgess of Old Aberdeen on 30 October 1820. [ACA]

GALL, ALEXANDER, born 1833 in Aberdeen, died at 79 State Street, Rochester, New York, on 2 August 1879. [AJ.17.9.1879]

GANSON, HERMAN, master of the Hope from Aberdeen to Miramachi, New Brunswick, in 1826, [NRS.E504.1.32]; master of the Bolivar of Aberdeen bound from Aberdeen with passengers for Quebec in 1835. [DPCA]; master of the Richibucto of Aberdeen trading between Aberdeen and Quebec in 1838, 1847, 1849, 1850, 1851, 1853, 1854, 1855 and 1858; master of the Jane Boyd of Aberdeen from Aberdeen with passengers bound for Quebec in 1854. [AJ][EEC][AH]

GARDEN, ALEXANDER, born 4 October 1794 in Aberdeen, was educated at King's College, Aberdeen, graduated MD in 1813, a surgeon in the service of the Honourable East India Company, died in Calcutta on 24 April 1845. [KCA][St Andrew's gravestone, Calcutta, India]

GARDEN, ALEXANDER, and Henrietta Coutts, both from Aberdeen, were married in Halifax, Nova Scotia, on 27 January 1824. [HJ.2.2.1824]

GARDNER, ALEXANDER, from Aberdeen, graduated MA from King's College, Aberdeen, on 31 March 1827, later a minister in Fergus, Canada. [KCA]

GARIOCH, ALEXANDER, a merchant in Aberdeen, died in 1802. [AJ.3.2.1802]

GARIOCH, ELIZABETH, in Aberdeen, relict of Reverend William Forbes in Airth, Stirlingshire, testament, 1790, Comm. Aberdeen. [NRS]

GARIOCH, Mrs MARY, born 1720, widow of Andrew Garioch a merchant in Aberdeen, died in 1810. [AJ.20.2.1810]

GARROW, WILLIAM, was admitted as an advocate burgess of Old Aberdeen on 30 October 1826. [ACA]

GARVOCK, ROBERT, son of James Garvock a salmon fisher and grandson of Alexander Davidson the burgess of guild, was apprenticed to Alexander Ferguson, a tailor in Aberdeen, from 1785 to 1790. [ACA]

GAULD, JOHN, was admitted as a wright burgess of Old Aberdeen on 21 April 1823. [ACA]

GEDDES, ALEXANDER COBHAM, a ship agent in Aberdeen, a victim of crime in 1825. [NRS.JC26.1825.29]

GEDDES, ANDREW, manager of the Aberdeen Lime Company, a victim of crime in 1825. [NRS.JC26.1825.29]

GEDDES, JOHN, clerk and apprentice of the Aberdeen Lime Company, a victim of crime in 1825. [NRS.JC26.1825.29]

GEDDES, JOHN, born 1822, arrived in Kingston, Jamaica, on 11 May 1841 on board the Rob Roy from Aberdeen. [TNA.CO140/33]

GEDDES, MARY ROBERTSON, youngest daughter of Andrew Geddes, a merchant in Aberdeen, married Francis G. Stanton a barrister at law, at York Place, Hamilton, Upper Canada, on 15 June 1838. [AJ.4724]; she died in Elora, Canada West, on 12 November 1850. [AJ.5370]

GERARD, Dr ALEXANDER, Professor of Divinity at King's College, Aberdeen, testament, 1795, Comm. Aberdeen. [NRS]

GERARD, ALEXANDER, second son of Dr Gilbert Gerard, Professor of Divinity at King's College, Aberdeen, a former Captain in Honourable East India Company Service, died at 6 Chanonry, Old Aberdeen, in 1839. [AJ.15.12.1839]

GERARD, JAMES, from Aberdeen, was educated at King's College, Aberdeen, in 1811, a surgeon in the Honourable East India Company Service. [KCA]

GERARD, JOHN, from Aberdeen, was educated at King's College, Aberdeen, in 1803, a surgeon in the Honourable East India Company Service. [KCA]

GERARD, Mrs, born 1761, widow of George Gerard jr. of Midstrath, and sister of Mrs Angus, died at 74 Dee Street, Aberdeen, in 1836. [AJ.14.11.1836]

GIBB, ADAM, a sailor in Aberdeen, husband of Janet Robson, 1792. [SPEBR]

GIBB, WILLIAM, was admitted as a burgess of Old Aberdeen on 26 July 1836. [ACA]

GIBBON, ALEXANDER, a skipper in Aberdeen, inventory, 1814, Comm. Aberdeen. [NRS]

GIBBON, HUGH, born 19 October 1812 in Aberdeen, died in Gorockpore, Bengal, India, on 19 November 1844. [Gorockpore gravestone]

GIBBON, ISABELLA, second daughter of James Gibbon in Aberdeen, married Alexander Morrice, a merchant, in Rio de Janeiro, Brazil, on 8 July 1809. [SM.72.798]

GIBBON, JAMES, born 1774, a merchant in Aberdeen, died there in 1848. [AJ.14.12.1848]

GIBBON, JOHN, born 22 November 1784, son of Alexander Gibbon, a mariner in Aberdeen, and his wife Isobel Duncan, was educated at King's College, Aberdeen, from 1798 to 1802, emigrated to Canada. [KCA]

GIBBON, REBECCA, relict of John Fraser a hosier in Aberdeen, testament, 1792, Comm. Aberdeen. [NRS]

GIBBIN, WILLIAM, jr., a skipper in Aberdeen, inventory, 1821, Comm. Aberdeen. [NRS]

GIBBIN, WILLIAM, the youngest, a skipper in Aberdeen, inventory, 1823, Comm. Aberdeen. [NRS]

GIBSON, JOHN, was admitted as a tailor burgess of Old Aberdeen on 29 October 1795. [ACA]

GIBSON, WILLIAM, son of William Gibson, was apprenticed to George Smith, a glazier in Aberdeen, from 1786 to 1790. [ACA]

GILCHRIST, ISAAC, in Aberdeen, graduated MD from King's College, Aberdeen, on 10 April 1845. [KCA]

GILES, JAMES, son of James Giles a painter in Aberdeen, a student at Marischal College in 1840, an artist who died in Rome. [MCA]

GILES, JOHN GORDON, youngest son of James Giles of the Royal Scottish Academy, died at 64 Bon Accord Street, Aberdeen, in 1834. [AJ.5.5.1834]

GILL, PATRICK, son of John Gill a lime merchant in Aberdeen, died in Richmond, Virginia, on 27 March 1852. [AJ.5.5.1852]

GILL, PETER, born 1757, a watchmaker, died in Union Terrace, Aberdeen, in 1850. [AJ.26.1.1850]

GILLESPIE, JAMES, born 1787 in Aberdeen, died in Montreal, Quebec, on 25 June 1821. [EA][S.240.272]

GLEGG, Captain, master of the Lion of Aberdeen from Peterhead to Quebec in 1858. [CM]

GLENNIE, ALEXANDER, was admitted as a trade burgess of Old Aberdeen on 30 October 1820. [ACA]

GLENNIE, CATHERINE, wife of Reverend Samuel McMillan, died at Rosemount Place, Aberdeen, in 1850. [AJ.17.12.1850]

GLENNIE, JOHN, was admitted as a burgess of Old Aberdeen on 29 October 1859. [ACA]

GOODBRAND, Mrs JESSEY, born in Aberdeen, died in Halifax, Nova Scotia, on 13 March 1821. [FP.15.3.1821]

GORDON, A., in North Lodge, Aberdeen, formerly a Captain of the Aberdeen Militia, applied to emigrate to Canada on 22 January 1827. [TNA.CO384.5.853]

GORDON, ADAM, born in Aberdeen, and Agnes Carr, eldest daughter of J. Carr in Dumfries, were married in Pictou, Nova Scotia, on 20 September 1823. [HJ.22.9.1823]

GORDON, or MCKAY, AMELIA JANE, in Mayville, Chautauqua, New York, daughter and heir of George Gordon a merchant in Aberdeen who died on 27 July 1850. [NRS.S/H]

GORDON, CAROLINE, in Mayville, Chautuaqua, New York, daughter and heir of George Gordon a merchant in Aberdeen who died 27 July 1850. [NRS.SH]

GORDON, CHARLES, of Wardhouse and Kildrummy, born 1749, died in Aberdeen in 1832. [AJ.23.12.1832]

GORDON, FRANCIS, son of John Gordon of Craig in Aberdeenshire, a writer in Aberdeen, was admitted as a Notary Public on 27 May 1791, [NRS.NP2.34.251]

GORDON, GEORGE, son of George Gordon, a blacksmith in Hardgate, Aberdeen, was apprenticed to William Littlejohn, a wright in Aberdeen, from 1789 to 1795. [ACA]

GORDON, GEORGE, a minister in Aberdeen, graduated DD from King's College, Aberdeen, on 23 October 1795. [KCA]

GORDON, GEORGE, born 1815, son of Adam Gordon of Cairnsfield, Aberdeen, died in Baltimore, Maryland, in 1861. [AJ.20.2.1861]

GORDON, GEORGE, born 1789, a surgeon in Bombay, India, died in Aberdeen on 4 May 1832. [St Nicholas gravestone, Aberdeen]

GORDON, HUNTLY, third daughter of William Gordon in Aberdeen, married Peter Ross from Demerara, in London on 16 June 1820. [BM.7.462][SM.86.94]

GORDON, ISABELLA, daughter of Charles Gordon an advocate, died in Aberdeen in 1823. [AJ.19.2.1823]

GORDON, JAMES, born 1793, son of George Gordon, [1701-1764], and his wife Elizabeth Irvine, [1710-1766], died in Jamaica on 29 August 1811. [St Nicholas gravestone, Aberdeen]

GORDON, JAMES, born 1800, died in Aberdeen in 1826. [AJ.29.1.1826]

GORDON, JAMES, son of Reverend James Gordon in Aberdeen, was educated at Marischal College around 1812. Later a surgeon in the service of the East India Company. [MCA]

GORDON, JAMES, born 1809, son of Nathaniel Gordon a manufacturer at Rippachy, Strathdon, a teacher, died at 246 George Street, Aberdeen, in 1846. [AJ.16.9.1846]

GORDON, JAMES, born 1790, a nurseryman and seedsman, died in Aberdeen in 1838. [AJ.27.4.1838]

GORDON, JANE, of Craigmyle, born 1751, died in Aberdeen in 1836. [AJ.4.1.1837]

GORDON, JESSIE, youngest daughter of Charles Gordon an advocate in Aberdeen, died there on 30 December 1825. [SM.97.255]

GORDON, JOHN, jr., an advocate in Aberdeen, testament, 1793, Comm. Aberdeen. [NRS]

GORDON, JOHN, a shipmaster in Aberdeen, father of Elizabeth Gordon, testament, 1797, Comm. Aberdeen. [NRS]

GORDON, Reverend JOHN, born 1760, a Roman Catholic clergyman, died in Aberdeen in 1823. [AJ.8.12.1823]

GORDON, LOUISA, born 1813, wife of James Irvine a brewer, died in Old Aberdeen, in 1844. [AJ.14.2.1844]

GORDON, MARGARET, daughter of Thomas Gordon the Professor of Philosophy at King's College, Aberdeen, testament, 1797, Comm. Aberdeen. [NRS]

GORDON, MARGARET ANN, youngest daughter of Reverend George Gordon in Keith, died in Old Aberdeen in 1811. [AJ.24.12.1811]

GORDON, ROBERT, son of James Gordon in Meldrum, was apprenticed to James Gordon a jeweller and goldsmith in Aberdeen on 26 October 1791. [ACA]

GORDON, ROBERT, son of John Gordon a mariner, was apprenticed to John Lamb, a wright in Aberdeen, from 1791 to 1796. [ACA]

GORDON, WILLIAM, born 1774, a book seller, died in Aberdeen in 1830. [AJ.22.5.1830]

GORDON, WILLIAM, born in Aberdeen, a fishing tackle manufacturer, died in Quebec on 8 August 1834. [AJ.4523]

GORDON, WILLIAM, born 1826, son of James Giles of the Royal Society of Art, died at 64 Bon Accord Street, Aberdeen, in 1845. [AJ.8.9.1845]

GORDON, Mrs, born 1759, widow of Lieutenant Colonel Gordon, died at 42 Bon Accord Street, Aberdeen, in 1842. [AJ.23.4.1842]

GRAHAM, JAMES, a prisoner in Aberdeen Tolbooth, was sentenced to be transported beyond the seas, on 16 April 1796. [NRS.JC11.42]

GRANT, BARBARA, widow of Alexander Robertson a saddler in America, sister and heir of Robert Charles Grant an advocate in Aberdeen, 1854. [NRS.S/H]

GRANT, CHARLES, born 1785, a Major of the 50th Regiment, died in Aberdeen in 1849. [AJ.2.6.1849]

GRANT, CHARLES LYALL, son of David Grant a merchant in Aberdeen, graduated MA from Marischal College in 1853, later a merchant in Shanghai, China. [MCA]

GRANT, MARY, wife of John Christie MD, died at 124 Union Street, Aberdeen, in 1850. [AJ.26.4.1850]

GRANT, PETER, master of the Spring of Aberdeen from Aberdeen with passengers bound for Quebec in 1811. [NRS.E504.1.24]

GRANT, ROBERT CHARLES, of Balgowan, born 1788, an advocate, died in Aberdeen in 1823. [AJ.23.3.1823]

GRANT, SAMUEL, a leather merchant in Aberdeen, testament, 1799, Comm. Aberdeen. [NRS]

GRANT, SUSAN, born 1753, wife of Reverend Bonniman in Premnay, died in Old Aberdeen in 1807. [AJ.29.7.1807]

GRASSIE, MARGARET, born 1820, arrived in Kingston, Jamaica, on 11 May 1841 on board the Rob Roy from Aberdeen. [TNA.CO140/33]

GRAY, ALEXANDER, master of the Amethyst of Aberdeen, from Aberdeen with passengers bound for Halifax, Nova Scotia, in 1815. [NRS.E504.1.25]

GRAY, ALEXANDER, born 1778, a rope and twine manufacturer, died at 77 West North Street, Aberdeen, in 1854. [AJ.10.3.1854]

GRAY, ANDREW, a skipper in Aberdeen, inventory, 1813, Comm. Aberdeen. [NRS]

GRAY, DAVID, Professor of Natural Philosophy in Aberdeen, died on 10 February 1856, father of Reverend David Thompson Gray, a chaplain in Nagpure, India. [NRS.S/H.1880]

GRAY, ELIZABETH, daughter of William Gray a merchant in Aberdeen, and wife of David White a tailor in Jamaica, 1793. [NRS.S/H]

GRAY, JOHN, born 1777, a shipmaster in Aberdeen, died on 17 January 1821. [Banchory Devenick gravestone, Kincardineshire]; inventory, 1821, Comm. Aberdeen. [NRS]

GRAY, JOHN, born 1743, for many years the schoolmaster of Old Machar and a magistrate of Old Aberdeen, died at King's College, Aberdeen, in 1818. [AJ.27.6.1818]

GRAY, JOHN, a merchant, died at 134 Crown Street, Aberdeen, in 1849. [AJ.20.4.1849]

GRAY, MARGARETTA SOPHIA, daughter of William Gray a printer in Montreal, Quebec, married James Webster, in Aberdeen on 26 February 1832. [AJ.4386]

GRAY, MARY, a prisoner in Aberdeen Tolbooth, was sentenced to be transported beyond the seas, on 14 September 1798 [NRS.JC11.43]

GRAY, ROBERT, was admitted as a weaver burgess of Old Aberdeen on 8 January 1801. [ACA]

GRAY, WILLIAM, from Aberdeen, proprietor of the 'Montreal Herald', died in Montreal, Quebec, on 5 May 1822. [BM.11.630]

GRAY, WILLIAM, jr., in Aberdeen, formerly a trader at the Bay of Chaleur, New Brunswick, in 1829. [NRS.CS17.1.46/555]

GREEN, GEORGE, was admitted as a meal seller burgess of Old Aberdeen on 16 February 1814. [ACA]

GREEN, GEORGE, son of John Green in Aberdeen, was educated at Marischal College, 1812-1815, later a farmer in Gartly. [MCA]

GREEN, JOHN, was admitted as a merchant burgess of Old Aberdeen on 28 October 1811. [ACA]

GREEN, JOHN, a builder, died at 90 Union Street, Aberdeen, in 1849. [AJ.23.6.1849]

GREENLAW, WILLIAM, born 1744, was crowned King of the Traveling Merchants in Kirkwall on 13 August 1830, died in Aberdeen in 1834. [AJ.24.5.1834]

GREENLAW, WILLIAM, son of William Greenlaw in Castlehill, Aberdeen, was apprenticed to James Gordon and Company, goldsmiths in Aberdeen, from 1787 to 1794. [ACA]

GREGORY, ANN, born 1775 in Aberdeen, relict of Ellis Roland a tinsmith, died in Montreal, Quebec, on 7 August 1851. [AJ.5408]

GRIGOR, ROBERT, agent of the Commercial Bank of Scotland in Aberdeen in 1849. [POD]

GRUB, ALEXANDER, was admitted as a shoemaker burgess of Old Aberdeen on 1 November 1819. [ACA]

GRUB, FRANCIS, was admitted as a burgess of Old Aberdeen on 31 October 1814. [ACA]

GRUB, GEORGE, was admitted as a shoemaker burgess of Old Aberdeen on 8 January 1801. [ACA]

GRUB, GEORGE, was admitted as a writer burgess of Old Aberdeen on 29 October 1832. [ACA]

GRUB, JAMES, was admitted as a shoemaker burgess of Old Aberdeen on 8 January 1801. [ACA]

GUNN, ALEXANDER, was admitted as a weaver burgess of Old Aberdeen on 25 January 1808. [ACA]

GUTHRIE, JOHN, a cooper and storekeeper in Aberdeen, was accused of embezzlement and reset in 1812. [NRS.AD14.12.100]

HACKET, CHARLES, born 1793, a merchant in Aberdeen, died in 1841. [AJ.14.10.1841]

HADDEN, DAVID, born 13 October 1773 in Aberdeen, son of Alexander Hadden and his wife Elspet Young, emigrated on the packet boat New Guide, landed in New York on 18 November 1806, a merchant in N.Y., died on 3 June 1856. [ANY]

HADDEN, JAMES, a sailor in Aberdeen, son of James Hadden a shipmaster there in 1798. [NRS.S/H]

HADDEN, WILLIAM INNES, son of Gavin Hadden in Aberdeen, was educated at Marischal College around 1824, later a merchant in Riga, Latvia. [MCA]

HALL, ALEXANDER, born 1760, a shipbuilder, died in Aberdeen in 1849. [AJ.2.3.1849]

HALL, Captain GEORGE, master of the Sisters of Aberdeen from Aberdeen to Quebec in 1839 and 1840. [AJ]

HALL, GEORGE, a house carpenter in Aberdeen, died 25 May 1835, his heir was his grandnephew Alexander Harvey Hall, formerly a Lieutenant of HM Indian Navy, then in Otago, New Zealand. [NRS.S/H]

HAMILTON, ROBERT, born 1742, Professor of Mathematics in Marischal College, Aberdeen, died in 1829. [AJ.14.7.1829]

HARPER, ALEXANDER, a baillie of Aberdeen, died at his house on the Green, Aberdeen, in 1838. [AJ.14.4.1838]

HARPER, or CARGILL, JANE SMITH, in Buffalo, New York, heir to her grandmother Jean Robertson, widow of John Smith in Aberdeen, who died on 13 November 1854. [NRS.S/H]

HARROW, ELSPET, formerly wife of George Harrow a stabler in Aberdeen, thereafter spouse to James Innes in the Gallowgait, Aberdeen, testament, 1791, Comm. Aberdeen. [NRS]

HARROW, MARGARET, daughter of Alexander Harrow a butcher in Aberdeen, versus James Jackson of the 94th Regiment of Foot, a Process of Divorce, 1816. [NRS.CC8.6.1599]

HARVEY, ELIZABETH, born 1760, widow of Alexander Gordon a physician in Aberdeen, died there in 1843. [AJ.8.3.1843]

HARVEY, ROBERT, of Braco, died in Aberdeen on 5 December 1825. [SM.97.128]

HARVEY, ROBERT, of Broomhill, Aberdeen, MD, died there in 1831. [AJ.19.6.1831]

HAY, ALEXANDER, from Aberdeen, a tutor in Virginia, later Rector of Antrim, Halifax County, Virginia, from 1790 until his death in 1819. [OD]

HAY, CHARLES, of Clifton Pen, Jamaica, died in Aberdeen on 14 August 1805. [SM.67.647]

HAY, ELIZABETH, widow of William Beet a blacksmith in Aberdeen, testament, 1791, Comm. Aberdeen. [NRS]

HAY, Reverend HUGH, in Aberdeen, and his sister Anna Hay, children of Dr James Hay, testament, 1793, Comm. Aberdeen. [NRS]

HAY, JAMES, of Monkshill, born 1775, died in Aberdeen in 1828. [AJ.14.2.1828]

HAY, JAMES, was admitted as a trade burgess of Old Aberdeen on 27 October 1817. [ACA]

HAY, JOHN, was admitted as a trade burgess of Old Aberdeen on 27 October 1817. [ACA]

HAY, Mrs MARGERY, born 1810, daughter of John Innes a merchant tailor in Aberdeen, died in Watertown, Jefferson County, New York, on 9 June 1848. [AJ.12.7.1848]

HAY, WILLIAM, was admitted as a stone merchant burgess of Old Aberdeen on 16 January 1830. [ACA]

HECTOR, ALEXANDER, was admitted as a merchant burgess of Old Aberdeen on 28 October 1805. [ACA]

HECTOR, ALEXANDER, son of William Hector, was admitted as a burgess of Old Aberdeen on 28 October 1811. [ACA]

HECTOR, JOHN, jr., son of William Hector, was admitted as a burgess of Old Aberdeen on 14 November 1799 [ACA]

HECTOR, JOHN, of Westfield, was admitted as a merchant burgess of Old Aberdeen on 14 November 1799. [ACA]

HECTOR, JOHN, was admitted as a merchant burgess of Old Aberdeen on 27 October 1817. [ACA]

HECTOR, WILLIAM, was admitted as a tanner burgess of Old Aberdeen on 22 April 1799. [ACA]

HECTOR, WILLIAM, was admitted as a merchant burgess of Old Aberdeen on 30 October 1799. [ACA]

HENDERSON, DAVID MITCHELL, son of William Henderson a builder in Aberdeen, was educated at Marischal College in 1859, later a missionary in Old Calabar, West Africa. [MCA]

HENDERSON, GEORGE, was admitted as a burgess of Old Aberdeen on 8 October 1808. [ACA]

HENDERSON, GEORGE, was admitted as a trade burgess of Old Aberdeen on 26 October 1818. [ACA]

HENDERSON, HELEN, daughter of Andrew Henderson MD in Aberdeen, died at Springbank Terrace, Aberdeen, in 1848. [AJ.18.10.1848]

HENDERSON, JAMES, was admitted as a merchant burgess of Old Aberdeen on 30 October 1820. [ACA]

HENDERSON, JAMES, eldest son of James Henderson, was admitted as a burgess of Old Aberdeen on 14 November 1835. [ACA]

HENDERSON, JOHN, in Aberdeen, was accused of housebreaking and theft in 1817. [NRS.AC17.14.40]

HENDERSON, JOHN, master of the Charlotte of Aberdeen from Aberdeen bound for Quebec in 1853. [AJ.5488]

HENDERSON, Mrs MARY, from Aberdeen, died on Johnson's Ranch, Bute County, USA, in 1851. [AJ.5420]

HENDERSON, P. B., from Aberdeen, married Henrietta J. Sweetlie. Eldest daughter of Simeon Sweetlie, in Kingston, Canada West, on 28 November 1850. [AJ.5370]

HENDERSON, WILLIAM, late Captain of the 4th Regiment of Foot, died in Aberdeen in 1809. [AJ.4.11.1809]

HENDERSON, WILLIAM, from Aberdeen, was educated at King's College, Aberdeen, in 1822, later a minister in Newcastle, New Brunswick. [KCA]

HENDERSON, Miss, only daughter of Captain Henderson of Newton, married John Miller of Trinidad, in Aberdeen in 1813. [EA.5198.263]

HENDRY, JOHN, a prisoner in Aberdeen Tolbooth, was banished from Scotland on 16 April 1796. [NRS.JC11.42]

HENRY, ANNE, wife of James Donaldson a merchant in Halifax, Nova Scotia, niece and heir of George Henry a merchant in Aberdeen who died on 3 March 1867. [NRS.S/H]

HENRY, CATHERINE, wife of Edward Allison a merchant in St John, New Brunswick, niece and heir of George Henry a merchant in Aberdeen who died on 3 March 1867. [NRS.S/H]

HENRY, JOHN, from Aberdeen, died in Halifax, Nova Scotia, in 1813. [GM.83.670][EA.5159.13]

HILL, JAMES, son of David Hill a merchant in Aberdeen, a student at Marischal College in 1840s, later a United Presbyterian minister in New Zealand. [MCA]

HILL, JOHN, in the Green of Aberdeen, testament, 1798, Comm. Aberdeen. [NRS]

HOBB, ANN, wife of John Hay a carver and guilder, died at 75 Union Street, Aberdeen, in 1844. [AJ.23.10.1844]

HOG, ANN, relict of James Scott a farmer in Baghadlie, in Hardgait, Aberdeen, testament, 1799, Comm. Aberdeen. [NRS]

HOGARTH, GEORGE, sr., born 1775, died at Crown Terrace, Aberdeen, in 1848. [AJ.27.4.1848]

HOGARTH, JOHN, son of George Hogarth a merchant in Aberdeen, was educated at Marischal College around 1830, later settled in Australia. [MCA]

HUDART, Mrs CATHERINE, in Aberdeen, relict of Andrew Lunan a glazier there, testament, 1796, Comm. Aberdeen. [NRS]

HUME, JOHN, a shipmaster in Aberdeen, testament 1798, Comm. Aberdeen. [NRS]

HUMPHREY, THOMAS, a shipmaster in Aberdeen, inventory, 1812, Comm. Aberdeen. [NRS]

HUNTER, ALEXANDER, was admitted as a trade burgess of Old Aberdeen in October 1816. [ACA]

HUNTER, ALEXANDER, was admitted as a merchant burgess of Old Aberdeen on 25 November 1825. [ACA]

HUNTER, GEORGE, born 1829 in Aberdeen died on Broadway, New York, on 7 December 1874. [AJ.30.12.1874]

HUNTER, JOHN CHALMERS, of Auchiries, born 1804, died in Aberdeen in 1823. [AJ.8.10.1823]

HUNTER, JOHN, was admitted as a burgess of Old Aberdeen on 28 October 1833. [ACA]

HUNTER, THOMAS, from St Nicholas parish, Aberdeen, was educated at King's College, Aberdeen, in 1852, a missionary in Bombay, India. [KCA.304]

HURD, JEAN, born 1808, a teacher, with Margaret Hurd, born 1828, William Hurd, born 1830, Arthur Hurd, born 1832, Elspeth Hurd, born 1835, Elizabeth Hurd, born 1836, and Charles Hurd, born 1840, arrived in Kingston, Jamaica, on 11 May 1841 on board the Rob Roy from Aberdeen. [TNA.CO140/33]

HUTCHEON, DAVID, an advocate, born 1765, died in Aberdeen in 1832. [AJ.10.12.1832]

HUTCHEON, JOHN, born 1835, son of William Hutcheon in Aberdeen, died in South Brooklyn, New York, on 19 August 1851. [AJ.5408]

IMLAY, ALEXANDER, was admitted as a trade burgess of Old Aberdeen on 13 November 1802. [ACA]

IMRIE, ALEXANDER, a manufacturer in Aberdeen, testament, 1800, Comm. Aberdeen. [NRS]

INGRAM, ALEXANDER, son of John Ingram, a labourer at Aberdeen brick-kilns, was apprenticed to George Watson, a baker in Aberdeen, from 1785 to 1790. [ACA]

INGRAM, ALEXANDER, was admitted as a merchant burgess of Old Aberdeen on 24 April 1827. [ACA]

INGRAM, ALEXANDER, a house carpenter in Aberdeen, father of John Ingram, born 1824, died in Washington City on 31 January 1866. [AJ.28.2.1866]

INNES, ALEXANDER, and ARTHUR, son of William Innes a merchant in Thurso, Caithness, residing in Aberdeen, testament, 1793, Comm. Aberdeen. [NRS]

INNES, ALEXANDER, of Breda, testament, 1798, Comm. Aberdeen. [NRS]

INNES, ALEXANDER, Commissary Clerk of Aberdeen, testament, 1790, Comm. Aberdeen. [NRS]

INNES, Mrs ELIZABETH, widow of John Cormack a mariner, in Aberdeen, testament, 1793, Comm. Aberdeen. [NRS]

INNES, Mrs ELIZABETH, widow of Thomas Gordon, Professor of Philosophy at King's College, Aberdeen, testament, 1799, Comm. Aberdeen. [NRS]

INNES, HELEN ELIZA, wife of William Boxil in Barbados, daughter and heir of Isabelle Lumsden or Innes in Aberdeen, in 1816. [NRS.S/H]

INNES, JAMES, was admitted as a trade burgess of Old Aberdeen on 18 January 1819. [ACA]

INNES, JAMES ROSE, graduated MA from King's College, Aberdeen, in 1822, later was Superintendent General of Education at the Cape of Good Hope, South Africa. [KCA]

INNES, JOHN, born 1771 in Aberdeen, master of the whaling ship Oscar of Aberdeen which was shipwrecked and he drowned off

Aberdeen on 1 April 1813, husband of Ann Mitchell born 1760, died 16 November 1828. [Newburgh gravestone, Aberdeenshire]

INNES, JOHN, born 1800, an architect, died at 41 Huntly Street, Aberdeen, in 1845. [AJ.19.7.1845]

INNES, MARGERY, daughter of John Innes a merchant tailor in Aberdeen, and wife of Alexander Hay, died in Watertown, Jefferson County, New York, on 9 June 1848. [AJ.5244]

INNES, THOMAS, son of Alexander Innes was admitted as a gardener burgess of Old Aberdeen on 30 October 1797. [ACA]

INNES, ..., born 1772, daughter of Alexander Innes of Cowie, wife of Alexander More, the Customs Collector of Aberdeen, died in Aberdeen in 1814. [AJ.9.1.1815]

INVERARITY, JOHN, born 11 November 1783, son of John Inverarity and his wife Henrietta Panton in Aberdeen, emigrated to Florida in 1802, a partner in the firm Panton, Leslie, and Company, and of John Forbes and Company, merchants, died 1854.

IRONSIDE, GEORGE EDMUND, born 1766 in Aberdeen, educated at King's College, Aberdeen, in 1781, married Helen ...., in Aberdeen, emigrated to New York in 1808, a teacher, died in Washington on 7 May 1827. [ANY]. Helen died in New York on 13 June 1815. [WC.30.6.1815]

IRVINE, ALEXANDER, was admitted as a burgess of Old Aberdeen on 14 November 1835. [ACA]

IRVINE, ALEXANDER, born 1776, died at 50 Castle Street, Aberdeen, in 1849. [AJ.19.12.1849]

IRVINE, ANN, relict of Colin Allan a goldsmith in Aberdeen, testament, 1799, Comm. Aberdeen. [NRS]

IRVINE, ANNE LOCH, daughter of Patrick Irvine of Inveramsay a Writer to the Signet, died in Aberdeen in 1830. [AJ.14.4.1830]

IRVINE, BARBARA, in Aberdeen, relict of Reverend Archibald Campbell at Grange, testament, 1795, Comm. Aberdeen. [NRS]

IRVINE, Dr CHARLES, formerly in St Thomas, Jamaica, later in Aberdeen, testament, 1794, Comm. Aberdeen. [NRS]

IRVINE, JAMES, was admitted as a burgess of Old Aberdeen on 8 October 1808. [ACA]

IRVINE, JOHN, a tanner at Well of Spa, Aberdeen, testament, 1798, Comm. Aberdeen. [NRS]

IRVINE, JOHN, formerly in Gothenburg, Sweden, later in Aberdeen, testament, 1795, Comm. Aberdeen. [NRS]

IRVINE, JOHN, born 1811, a labourer, arrived in Kingston, Jamaica, on 11 May 1841 on board the Rob Roy from Aberdeen. [TNA.CO140/33]

IRVINE, Dr JOHN, born 1742 in Aberdeen, died in Savanna, Georgia, on 15 October 1808. [Savanna Death Register]

IRVINE, JOHN, in Old Aberdeen, graduated MD from King's College, Aberdeen, on 13 April 1813. [KCA]

IRVINE, JOHN, jr., was admitted as a merchant burgess of Old Aberdeen on 30 October 1797, [ACA]; a merchant who died in Old Aberdeen in 1829. [AJ.30.9.1829]

IZAT, DAVID, son of D. Izat, a shipmaster in Aberdeen, was apprenticed to James Gordon, a goldsmith in Aberdeen, from 1786 to 1793. [ACA], died in Aberdeen in 1800. [ACA]

JACKSON, Captain GEORGE, from Aberdeen, died in Quebec on 3 May 1877. [EC.28901]

JACKSON, SAMUEL, a servant from Aberdeen, settled by the Swan River, Australia, by 1830. [BPP]

JAFFREY, WILLIAM, born 1789 in Aberdeen, a gardener who died in St John, New Brunswick, on 22 February 1827. [CG.1.3.1827]

JAMIESON, ALEXANDER, clerk to Hugh Gordon and Company merchants in Aberdeen, testament, 1797, Comm. Aberdeen. [NRS]

JAMIESON, CHARLES, a gentleman from London, now in Aberdeen, testament, 1791, Comm. Aberdeen. [NRS]

JAMIESON, GEORGE, a gardener in Aberdeen, testament, 1796, Comm. Aberdeen. [NRS]

JAMIESON, JAMES, in Aberdeen, a sailor in the Royal Navy, inventory, 1817, Comm. Aberdeen. [NRS]

JAMIESON, JANET, spouse to John Kirktown formerly a woolcomber in Spittal, later a soldier of the Aberdeenshire Regiment, testament, 1795, Comm. Aberdeen. [NRS]

JAMIESON, JOHN, was admitted as a shoemaker burgess of Old Aberdeen on 26 October 1835. [ACA]

JAMIESON, WILLIAM, was admitted as a merchant burgess of Old Aberdeen on 31 October 1814. [ACA]

JAMIESON, Captain, master of the Lion of Aberdeen from Aberdeen to Quebec in 1856. [AJ]

JEANS, JOHN, was admitted as a mariner burgess of Old Aberdeen on 26 October 1829. [ACA]

JEANS, WILLIAM DUTHIE B., a merchant in Montreal, son of John Jeans, [1790-1849], a shipmaster in Aberdeen, and his wife Susan Baxter, 1791-1859]. [St Clement's gravestone, Aberdeen]; grandson and heir to John Baxter a boatman in Aberdeen who died on 4 December 1847. [NRS.S/H]

JOHNSTON, ANDREW, master of the Alert of Aberdeen from Aberdeen with passengers bound for Quebec in 1812. [QM]

JOHNSTON, GEORGE, was admitted as a merchant burgess of Old Aberdeen on 14 November 1799. [ACA]

JOHNSTON, GEORGE, MD, born 1791 in Aberdeen, died in Pictou, Nova Scotia, in July 1830. [AR.31.7.1830]

JOHNSTON, JAMES, formerly in the Mains of Ardo, later in Old Aberdeen, testament, 1800, Comm. Aberdeen. [NRS]

JOHNSTON, JAMES, sr., born 1780, a merchant, died at 62 Dee Street, Aberdeen, in 1847. [AJ.23.4.1847]

JOHNSTON, JAMES, a merchant in Aberdeen later in USA, father of William Johnston on Honourable East India Company Service in 1856. [NRS.S/H]

JOHNSTONE, MARGARET, second daughter of Alexander Johnstone of North Broadford, Aberdeen, married Arthur Simpson of Brant, Bruce County, Canada West, in Toronto on 14 November 1861. [AJ.5940]

JOHNSTON, WILLIAM, born 1749, a merchant in Aberdeen, died in 1830. [AJ.9.11.1830]

JOHNSTON, WILLIAM, of Viewfield, born 1761, a merchant in Aberdeen, died in 1831. [AJ.22.2.1832]

JOYNER, ALEXANDER, a tailor in Aberdeen, testament, 1798, Comm. Aberdeen. [NRS]

JOINER, DANIEL, born 1751, a teacher in Skene Square, Aberdeen, died in 1826. [AJ.29.9.1826]

JOYNER, ELIZABETH, daughter of James Masson in Aberdeen, heir to her brother Robert Joyner in Baltimore, Maryland, in 1810. [NRS.S/H]

JOPP, CHARLES MITCHELL, in Keith Hall, Jamaica, nephew and heir of Jean Jopp, widow of Gavin Young a merchant in Aberdeen, 1837. [NRS.S/H]

JOPP, JAMES, of Cotton, a merchant and former Provost of Aberdeen, testament, 1794, Comm. Aberdeen. [NRS]

JOPP, JEAN, born 1754, widow of Gavin Young, died in Aberdeen in 1836. [AJ.1836]

JOPP, ROBERT, son of Andrew Jopp an advocate in Aberdeen, a student at Marischal College around 1825, later a farmer in New Zealand. [MCA]

JOSS, JAMES, master of the <u>Jane Geary of Aberdeen</u> from Aberdeen with passengers bound for Port Philip, Victoria, Australia, on 24 September 1852, landed in Melbourne, Victoria, on 20 January 1853. [AJ.5453/5478]

KEARD, ..., born 1776, 'for upwards of 44 years Precentor of Trinity Church', died in Aberdeen in 1843. [AJ.2.10.1843]

KEITH, ALEXANDER, was admitted as a burgess of Old Aberdeen on 1 October 1810. [ACA]

KEITH, ALEXANDER, son of Alexander Keith, was admitted as a painter burgess of Old Aberdeen on 30 September 1833. [ACA]

KEITH, FRASER, was admitted as a weaver burgess of Old Aberdeen on 22 April 1811. [ACA]

KEITH, GEORGE, in Aberdeen, brother and heir of James Keith in La Chine, Quebec, later in Aberdeen, who died 27 January 1851. [NRS.S/H]

KEITH, GEORGE SILVER, son of William Keith MD in Aberdeen, a student at Marischal College in 1850s, later Lieutenant Colonel of the Madra Staff Corps in India. [MCA]

KEITH, JAMES, born 1783, of the Hudson Bay Company, died at 101 Crown Street, Aberdeen, in 1851. [AJ.27.1.1851]

KEITH, JAMES, born 1775, a surgeon of the Royal Navy, died at 1 Crown Place, Aberdeen, in 1851. [AJ.22.2.1851]

KEITH, WILLIAM, a surgeon of Union Place, Aberdeen, married Mary Croom, only daughter o George Croom a merchant in Monifieth, in Dundee on 27 December 1825. [SM.97.254]

KELMAN, WILLIAM, born 1832 in Keyhead, Aberdeenshire, third son of John Kelman, died at 2 Granite Street, Boston, USA, on 16 October 1872. [AJ.6513]

KEMLO, WILLIAM, born 1802, a labourer in Aberdeen, was accused of assault in Turriff in 1835. [NRS.AD14.35.70]

KERR, GEORGE, born 1770, a surgeon, died in Aberdeen in 1826. [AJ.21.3.1826]

KERR, THOMAS, from Aberdeen, married Sarah Jane Jacox, youngest daughter of Thomas Jacox, in Saltspringville, Montgomery County, New York, on 1 October 1845. [AJ.5105]

KERR, WILLIAM, aged 14 months, son of Thomas Kerr in Sharon, Wisconsin, from Aberdeen, died on 18 September 1847. [AJ.5207]

KIDD, WILLIAM CAMPBELL, MA, born 1796, eldest son of Reverend James Kidd, Professor of Oriental Languages in Marischal College, Aberdeen, graduated MA from Marischal College in 1813, a minister who died in Richmond, Virginia, on 31 August 1825. [MCA] [AJ.31.8.1825][EA] [BM.18.780]

KILGOUR, ALEXANDER, late lecturer in Aberdeen, an honorary graduate, MD, from King's College, Aberdeen, on22 June 1849. [KCA]

KING, JAMES, was admitted as a merchant burgess of Old Aberdeen on 1 November 1797. [ACA]

KING, JESSIE, daughter of Charles King in Aberdeen, married Reverend Charles Anderson, MA, of Richmond, Cape Colony, at Bon Accord Cottage, Wynberg, Cape Town, Cape of Good Hope, South Africa, on 12 May 1864, [AJ.6078]

KNIGHT, JAMES, born 1803, died in Aberdeen on 22 December 1843, brother of Alexander Knight in Halifax, Nova Scotia. [Halifax Times: 23.1.1844]

KNIGHT, Dr WILLIAM, born in Aberdeen, Professor of Moral Philosophy at the University of Georgetown, died in Georgetown, Kentucky, on 1 March 1837. [DPCA.1826]

KNIGHT, WILLIAM, LLD, born 1786, Professor of Natural Philosophy at Marischal College, Aberdeen, died there in 1844. [AJ.3.12.1844]

KNIGHT, WILLIAM, born 1828, second son of Dr Knight of Marischal College, Aberdeen, died at Springbank Terrace, Aberdeen, in 1850. [AJ.11.6.1850]

KYNOCH, NINIAN, was admitted as a merchant burgess of Old Aberdeen on 30 October 1814. [ACA]

KYNOCH, NINIAN, in Spittal, was admitted as a merchant burgess of Old Aberdeen on 29 September 1834. [ACA]

LAIDLAW, WILLIAM, a merchant in Halifax, Nova Scotia, later in Ship Row, Aberdeen, died there on 20 February 1833. [AJ.4442]

LAING, Mrs ELIZABETH, wife of William Laing MD, died at 7 Golden Square, Aberdeen, in 1853. [AJ.1.12.1853]

LAING, JAMES MCGREGOR, a surgeon in USA, son and heir of William Laing a physician in Aberdeen who died on 22 August 1862. [NRS.S/H]

LAING, JOHN, was admitted as a merchant burgess of Old Aberdeen on 29 October 1798. [ACA]

LAING, JOHN, was admitted as a trade burgess of Old Aberdeen on 23 August 1823. [ACA]

LAING, ROBERT, was admitted as a trade burgess of Old Aberdeen on 17 March 1807. [ACA]

LAING, WILLIAM, son of Dr William Laing in Aberdeen, graduated MA from Marischal College in 1845, later in India. [MCA]

LAING, Captain, master of the Morningfield of Aberdeen from Tobermory with passengers bound for Pictou, Nova Scotia, on 26 July 1819. [NRS.E504.35.2]

LAIRD, JAMES, a skipper in Aberdeen, inventory, 1823, Comm. Aberdeen. [NRS]

LAMB, R., master of the Hibernia of Aberdeen from Quebec to Aberdeen in 1816. [NRS.E504.33.3]; master of the Heroine of Aberdeen from Dundee with passengers bound for New York in 1831, also in 1832. [DPCA.1511/1559]

LAMONT, BARBARA, widow of Dwight Bishop in Stratford, Connecticut, niece and heir of Margaret Lamont in Aberdeen who died in January 1833. [NRS.S/H]

LAMONT, HELEN, wife of William McGarth in Stratford, Connecticut, niece and heir of Margaret Lamont in Aberdeen who died in January 1833. [NRS.S/H]

LAMONT, PATRICK B., born 1787 in Aberdeen, a painter in New York from 1818, died on 7 May 1828. [ANY]

LAURENCE, ISOBEL, in Aberdeen, testament, 1798, Comm. Aberdeen. [NRS]

LAW, GEORGE, a salmon fisher at the Bridgend of Don, Aberdeenshire, testament, 1793, Comm. Aberdeen. [NRS]

LAW, WILLIAM, was found guilty of housebreaking in Aberdeen in 1814 and sentenced to transportation to the colonies for 14 years. [NRS.GD1.959]

LAWRENCE, JAMES, born 1786, a manufacturer in Aberdeen, died in 1842. [AJ.10.4.1842]

LAWRENCE, ALEXANDER, born 1823, a labourer, arrived in Kingston, Jamaica, on 11 May 1841 on board the Rob Roy from Aberdeen. [TNA.CO140/33]

LAWRIE, BARBARA, wife of James Hogg in Canada West, daughter and heir to David Lawrie a comb manufacturer in Aberdeen who died on 8 November 1858. [NRS.S/H]

LAWS, GEORGE, was admitted as a wright burgess of Old Aberdeen on 12 February 1854. [ACA]

LAWS, ROBERT, was admitted as a wright burgess of Old Aberdeen on 27 August 1839. [ACA]

LAWS, WILLIAM, was admitted as a cartwright burgess of Old Aberdeen on 1 October 1829. [ACA]

LAWSON, ALEXANDER, was admitted as a blacksmith burgess of Old Aberdeen on 15 November 1794. [ACA]

LAWSON, ANDREW, was admitted as a merchant burgess of Old Aberdeen on 30 October 1825. [ACA]

LAWSON, FRANCIS, was admitted as a burgess of Old Aberdeen on 28 October 1811. [ACA]

LAWSON, JAMES, a skipper in Aberdeen, inventory, 1821, Comm. Aberdeen. [NRS]

LAWSON, JOHN, was admitted as a merchant burgess of Old Aberdeen on 1 October 1829. [ACA]

LAWSON, JOHN, MD, born 1812 in Aberdeen, Mayor of Paris, Ontario, died there on 8 May 1875. [EC.28288]

LEASK, GEORGE, an advocate, died in Aberdeen in 1845. [AJ.10.3.1842]

LEASK, LYELL, was admitted as a burgess of Old Aberdeen on 14 November 1835. [ACA]

LEASK, REBECCA URQUHART, from Old Aberdeen, married Peter L. Sutherland, the Surgeon General, in Durban, Natal, South Africa, on 31 January 1857. [EEC.21067]; she died in Pietermaritzburg, Natal, on 17 January 1862. [AJ.5960]

LEASK, ROBERT, born 1814, formerly a skipper in Aberdeen, died in Cape Town, Cape of Good Hope, South Africa, in 1856. [AJ.5678]

LEASK, THOMAS, was admitted as a merchant burgess of Old Aberdeen on 9 September 1822. [ACA]

LEIGHTON, JOHN, was admitted as a trade burgess of Old Aberdeen on 27 August 1823. [ACA]

LEITCH, WILLIAM, was admitted as a blacksmith burgess of Old Aberdeen on 25 January 1802. [ACA]

LEITH, ALEXANDER, a master of Aberdeen Grammar School, testament, 1799, Comm. Aberdeen. [NRS]

LEITH, JOHN, a surgeon in Spanish Town, Jamaica, son of James Leith of Whiterigside, appointed his uncle Laurence Leith of Bucharn and William Burnet an advocate in Aberdeen as his factors, in 1790. [NRS.RD4.243.1183]

LENDRUM, JANET, widow of John Bisset a merchant in Aberdeen, died at 125 Crown Street, Aberdeen, in 1852. [AJ.11.2.1852]

LESLIE, ALEXANDER, of Berryden, a merchant in Aberdeen, testament, 1800, Comm. Aberdeen. [NRS]

LESLIE, Captain ALEXANDER, master of the Albion of Aberdeen from Aberdeen with passengers bound for Halifax, Miramachi, Pictou, or St John, in 1831, 1833, 1834, 1835, 1836, 1837, 1838, 1839, 1840, 1843, 1846, 1847, 1849, 1850, 1851, and 1853. [AJ][EEC][PANS]

LESLIE, ALEXANDER JAMES, son of Alexander Leslie in Aberdeen, was educated at Marischal College in 1856, later a sheep farmer in Australia. [MCA]

LESLIE, CHRISTIAN, born 1762, widow of Alexander Burnett of Kemnay, died in Old Aberdeen, in 1842. [AJ.14.2.1842]

LESLIE, GEORGE, formerly in Borrowstoun, Newhills, later in Aberdeen, testament, 1791, Comm. Aberdeen. [NRS]

LESLIE, GEORGE, in Bithnie, Forbes, Aberdeenshire, testament, 1791, Comm. Aberdeen. [NRS]

LESLIE, GEORGE, at Bridge of Don, was admitted as a burgess of Old Aberdeen on 10 November 1792. [ACA]

LESLIE, GEORGE, formerly in Jamaica, later in Old Aberdeen, testament, 1796, Comm. Aberdeen. [NRS]

LESLIE, GEORGE, was admitted as a trade burgess of Old Aberdeen on 13 November 1802. [ACA]

LESLIE, HELEN, born 1768, daughter of John Leslie the Professor of Greek in King's College, Aberdeen, died in Don Street, Old Aberdeen, in 1853. [AJ.19.7.1853]

LESLIE, HUGH FRASER, in Jamaica, son and heir of Hugh Leslie of Powis, Aberdeen, who died 8 April 1812; also, brother and heir of John Leslie of Powis in Aberdeen who died on 27 November 1847. [NRS.S/H]

LESLIE, ISABELLA, youngest daughter of John Leslie in Aberdeen, married William Sutherland MB, in Port Elizabeth, Cape of Good Hope, South Africa, on 30 May 1867. [AJ.6237]

LESLIE, JAMES, was admitted as a trade burgess of Old Aberdeen on 28 September 1818. [ACA]

LESLIE, JOHN, at Bridge of Don, was admitted as a burgess of Old Aberdeen on 10 November 1792. [ACA]

LESLIE, JOHN, born 1765, son of John Leslie and his wife Helen Ker in Aberdeen, a soldier from 1782 until 1813, Major of the 5th Native Infantry in the Bengal Army, died in Rewah, India, on 2 December 1813. [BA.3.45]

LESLIE, JOHN, was admitted as a trade burgess of Old Aberdeen on 13 November 1802. [ACA]

LESLIE, JOHN, was admitted as a trade burgess of Old Aberdeen on 28 October 1811. [ACA]

LESLIE, JOHN, born 1821 in Aberdeen, died in South Africa on 13 December 1883. [St George gravestone, Port Elizabeth, Cape of Good Hope, South Africa]

LESLIE, MARGARET, daughter of William Leslie, a merchant in Aberdeen, married George Duncan from Port Elizabeth, at Uitenhage, Cape of Good Hope, South Africa, on 28 March 1864. [AJ.6074]

LESLIE, ROBERT, son of William Leslie in Aberdeen, settled in Grenada, died on 9 October 1818. [EA.5743.31]

LESLIE, WILLIAM, son of James Leslie in Aberdeen, died in St Lucie, Jamaica, on 7 August 1818. [S.94.18]

LESLIE, Reverend WILLIAM, third son of Hugh Leslie of Powis, was drowned in the Bishop's Loch, New Machar, in 1853. [AJ.9.7.1853]

LESLIE, WILLIAM, was admitted as a shoemaker burgess of Old Aberdeen on 25 October 1856. [ACA]

LESSEL, ROBERT, a skipper in Aberdeen, inventory, 1811, Comm. Aberdeen. [NRS]

LEVIE, WILLIAM, son of William Levie a sailor, was apprenticed to George Strachan, a shoemaker in Aberdeen, from 1784 to 1794. [ACA]

LEYS, JOHN, born 1791 in Aberdeen, an engineer, emigrated to Toronto in 1826, died in St Croix, Danish West Indies, on 8 April 1846. [AJ.5133]

LICKLEY, WILLIAM, a cartwright in the Gallowgait, Aberdeen, testament, 1790, Comm. Aberdeen. [NRS]

LIGERTWOOD, THOMAS, born 1767, a merchant, died in Aberdeen in 1837. [AJ.27.11.1837]

LIGERTWOOD, WILLIAM, of Logierieve, died in Aberdeen in 1851. [AJ.13.10.1851]

LINTON, ALEXANDER, was admitted as a baker burgess of Old Aberdeen on 25 October 1856. [ACA]

LINTON, WILLIAM, was admitted as a merchant burgess of Old Aberdeen on 27 August 1823. [ACA]

LISTER, ALEXANDER, was admitted as a trade burgess of Old Aberdeen on 27 October 1817. [ACA]

LITTLEJOHN, WILLIAM, born 1731, a merchant, house builder, and magistrate in Aberdeen, died in 1806. [AJ.13.6.1806]

LITTLEJOHN, WILLIAM, cashier of the Aberdeen and County Bank in Aberdeen in 1849. [POD]

LIVINGSTON, CHRISTIAN, a mariner aboard the *Mary* in Aberdeen harbour, testament, 1798, Comm. Aberdeen. [NRS]

LIVINGSTONE, ISABELL, youngest daughter of Dr Livingstone in Aberdeen, married Dr Thomas Pye Weeks, a physician in Nevis, on 21 April 1789, [SM.51.361]; she died on Nevis on 14 November 1792. [SM.55.50]

LIVINGSTONE, LILLIAS, daughter of Dr Thomas Livingstone a physician in Aberdeen, died in Liverpool in 1829. [AJ.24.2.1829]

LOBHAM, ELIZABETH, born 1818, a servant, arrived in Kingston, Jamaica, on 11 May 1841 on board the Rob Roy from Aberdeen. [TNA.CO140/33]

LOGAN, JAMES, master of the Hunter of Aberdeen from Aberdeen with passengers bound for Halifax, Nova Scotia, in May 1817. [NRS.E504.1.27]

LONGMUIR, COLIN MILNE, son of Reverend John Longmuir in Aberdeen, was educated at Marischal College in 1859, later a banker in Melbourne, Victoria, Australia, married Kate Campbell in St Kilda, Melbourne, in 1875. [MCA][AJ.6667]

LONGMUIR, JOHN, master of the Curlew of Aberdeen died in Riga, Latvia, on 19 August 1848. [SG.1744]

LOW, ALEXANDER, a merchant in Aberdeen, died on 26 February 1863, grandfather of Alexander Low McEwan in Essequibo, British Guiana. [NRS.S/H]

LOW, GEORGE, a blacksmith in Aberdeen, and his wife Isobel Orchardton, testament, 1790, Comm. Aberdeen. [NRS]

LOW, JAMES, born 8 March 1759 in Aberdeen, son of John Low, was educated at Utrecht University, a tutor in Rotterdam and in Utrecht, a minister in the Netherlands from 1783, died on 20 November 1817. [F.7.539]

LUMSDEN, CLEMENT, born 1796, a Writer to the Signet and an Advocate, died at 17 Albyn Place, Aberdeen, in 1853. [AJ.27.11.1853]

LUMSDEN, or INNES, ISABELLA, in Aberdeen, mother of Helen Eliza Innes, wife of William Boxil in Barbados, 1816. [NRS.S/H]

LUNAN, JAMES, was admitted as a trade burgess of Old Aberdeen on 27 October 1817. [ACA]

LUNAN, JAMES, was admitted as a watchmaker burgess of Old Aberdeen on 26 October 1818. [ACA]

LUTHOOD, JAMES, victim of bigamy in Aberdeen, 1817. [NRS.AD14.17.156]

MCANDREW, JOHN, master of the Sir William Wallace of Aberdeen from Aberdeen with passengers bound for Quebec in 1855 and 1856. [DPCA]

MCCALLAN, JAMES, probably from Aberdeen, a merchant in Halifax, Nova Scotia, died on 8 May 1815, probate 8 May 1815, Halifax, Nova Scotia.

MCCOMBIE, MARGARET, born 1805, widow of Simpson Duguid of Cammachmore, died at 86 Crown Street, Aberdeen, in 1854. [AJ.26.11.1854]

MCCOMBIE, PETER, of Lynturk, born 1767, a merchant in Aberdeen, died in 1832. [AJ.4.1.1833]

MCCRAW, JOHN, a seaman in Aberdeen, was accused of housebreaking and theft in 1817. [NRS.AC17.14.40]

MCCREERY, JOHN, born 1822, from Aberdeen, died in New York on 1 February 1860. [AJ.5851; 29.2.1860

MCCRINDELL, THOMAS, born 1794 in Aberdeen, son of George McCrindell and his wife Margaret Cruickshank, emigrated via London aboard the Venus bound for New York on 27 April 1822, a merchant there from 1822 to 1837. [ANY]

MACCULLUM, Reverend JOHN, from Aberdeen, died in the Red River Colony, Hudson Bay, on 3 October 1849. [GM.NS33.546]

MCDONALD, ALEXANDER, in Aberdeen, a former Captain of the Florida Rangers, probate, April 1805, PCC. [TNA]

MCDONALD, ANGUS, a farmer in Nova Scotia, brother of Hugh McDonald a merchant in Aberdeen, 1812. [NRS.S/H]

MCDONALD, CHARLES, from Aberdeen, was educated at King's College, Aberdeen, graduated MA in 1850, later a Professor of Mathematics in Halifax, Nova Scotia. [KCA]

MCDONALD, GILBERT, was admitted as a burgess of Old Aberdeen on 27 October 1817. [ACA]

MCDONALD, GILBERT, an apothecary and general practitioner in medicine, died in Old Aberdeen in 1833. [AJ.15.5.1833]

MCDONALD, JAMES, was admitted as a wright burgess of Old Aberdeen on 26 September 1803. [ACA]

MACDONALD, JAMES, master of the Bolivar of Aberdeen from Dundee to Charleston, South Carolina, and Savannah, Georgia, in 1830. [DPCA.1432/1479]

MCDONALD, JAMES, born 1796, a millwright, arrived in Kingston, Jamaica, on 11 May 1841 on board the Rob Roy from Aberdeen. [TNA.CO140/33]

MCDONALD, JESSIE, second daughter of James McDonald on Aberdeen, married Peter Geddes a bank manager in Chicago, Illinois, in New York on 23 May 1862. [AJ.5970]

MCDONALD, JOHN, was admitted as a burgess of Old Aberdeen on 27 October 1817. [ACA]

MCDOUGAL, ANN, born 1800, of Sim's Square, St Nicholas, Aberdeen, was accused of concealment of pregnancy in 1823. [NRS.AD14.23.204]

MCDOWAL, ANDREW, was admitted as a seedsman burgess of Old Aberdeen on 24 December 1798. [ACA]

MCGILLIVRAY, PAUL HOWARD, son of Professor McGillivray, was educated at Marischal College in 1847, graduated MA in 1851, later a surgeon in Williamston, Victoria, Australia. [MCA]

MCGILLIVRAY, WILLIAM, LL.D., Professor of Natural History at Marischal College, Aberdeen, died at 67 Crown Street, Aberdeen, in 1852. [AJ.5.9.1852]

MCGREGOR, WILLIAM, was admitted as a baker burgess of Old Aberdeen on 26 October 1867. [ACA]

MCGRIGOR, JOHN, born 1758 in Aberdeen, died in Lunenburg, Nova Scotia, on 4 April 1842. [AR:16.4.1842]

MCHARDY, DAVID, was admitted as a blacksmith burgess of Old Aberdeen on 26 October 1812. [ACA]

MCHARDY, DAVID, was admitted as a trade burgess of Old Aberdeen on 22 December 1823. [ACA]

MCHARDY, DAVID, jr., was admitted as a trade burgess of Old Aberdeen on 23 November 1866. [ACA]

MCHARDY, JOHN, born 1752, for many years a nurseryman at Auchmull, died in Aberdeen in 1836. [AJ.6.1.1837]

MCHARDY, JOHN, was admitted as a trade burgess of Old Aberdeen in October 1816. [ACA]

MCHARDY, JOHN, was admitted as a trade burgess of Old Aberdeen on 22 December 1823. [ACA]

MCHATTIE, ANN, daughter of John McHattie a merchant in Aberdeen, married Reverend John Tawse, MA, a missionary of the Presbytery of Toronto, on 9 August 1836. She died on 22 June 1841 at Mansfield Cottage, King Home District, Upper Canada. [AJ.4623/ 4882]

MACHRAY, GEORGE, son of Robert Machray, a dyer in Old Aberdeen, apprenticed to Margaret Morice and Company in Aberdeen, from 1789 to 1794. [ACA]

MACHRAY, JAMES, son of Robert Machray, was admitted as a dyer burgess of Old Aberdeen on 2 November 1807. [ACA]

MACHRAY, PATRICK, born in Aberdeen, eldest son of Robert Machray a manufacturer, a merchant in Demerara, a deed, 1824, [NRS.RD5.275.8]; died in Georgetown, Demerara, in 1835. [AJ.22.7.1835]

MACHRAY, ROBERT, son of Robert Machray, a dyer in Old Aberdeen, apprenticed to William Donald a baker in Aberdeen, from 1790 to 1795, [ACA]; was admitted as a baker burgess of Old Aberdeen on 21 April 1800. [ACA]

MACHRAY, ROBERT, from Aberdeen, was educated at King's College, Aberdeen, in 1851, later Primate of Canada. [KCA.303]

MCINNES, CHARLES, eldest son of George McInnes in Old Aberdeen, died in St Thomas in the Vale, Jamaica, in December 1828. [BM.25.684]

MCINTOSH, JAMES, born 1804, a carpenter, with Elspeth McIntosh, born 1802, Elizabeth McIntosh, born 1823, Jean McIntosh, born 1827, and Isabella McIntosh, born 1829, arrived in Kingston, Jamaica, on 11 May 1841 on board the Rob Roy from Aberdeen. [TNA.CO140/33]

MCINTOSH, WILLIAM, born 1814, a labourer, with Mary McIntosh, born 1817, and Isabella, born 1840, arrived in Kingston, Jamaica, on 11 May 1841 on board the Rob Roy from Aberdeen. [TNA.CO140/33]

MACKAY, HUGH, a tailor in Aberdeen, father of William Mackay who died in Yonkers, New York, on 21 February 1875. [AJ.7.4.1875]

MCKAY, JEAN, in College Street, Aberdeen, was accused of housebreaking and theft in 1817. [NRS.AC17.14.40]

MCKAY, JOHN, master of the Silastria of Aberdeen from Leith with passengers bound for Melbourne, Victoria, Australia, on 6 April 1859, landed there on 3 August 1859. [AJ.5804/5831]

MCKENZIE, ALEXANDER, Lieutenant of HM'S 4TH Ceylon Regiment, died at Loanhead, Aberdeen, on 3 November 1825. [SM.97.127]

MCKENZIE, CATHERINE, born 1829, arrived in Kingston, Jamaica, on 11 May 1841 on board the Rob Roy from Aberdeen. [TNA.CO140/33]

MACKENZIE, CHARLES, was admitted as a burgess of Old Aberdeen on 12 November 1804. [ACA]

MCKENZIE, DAVID, from the Poor Hospital in Aberdeen, was apprenticed to David Wyllie, a tailor in Aberdeen, from 1786 to 1792. [ACA]

MACKENZIE, GEORGE, was admitted as a shoemaker burgess of Old Aberdeen on 12 November 1804. [ACA]

MCKENZIE, JOHN, a skipper in Aberdeen, inventory, 1812, Comm. Aberdeen. [NRS]

MCKENZIE, SIMON, from Old Machar, Aberdeen, was educated at King's College, Aberdeen, in 1848, a minister in Brisbane, Queensland, Australia. [KCA]

MCKENZIE, WILLIAM MASON, in Charleston, USA, heir to his grand-aunt Jane Mavor, wife of John Grant in Birchfield, Aberdeen, who died on 28 January 1846. [NRS.S/H]

MACKENZIE, WILLIAM RATTRAY, in Canada, brother and heir of Jemima Mackenzie in Aberdeen, 1847. [NRS.S/H]

MACKEY, ALEXANDER, from Aberdeen, graduated MA from King's College, Aberdeen, on 25 March 1814, later was a minister in Amsterdam, Holland. [KCA]

MACKIE, ALEXANDER, a merchant in Aberdeen, sederunt book, 1821. [NRS.CS96.1252]

MACKIE, ANDREW, son of William Mackie a merchant in Aberdeen, graduated MA from Marischal College in 1823, later a Major of the Spanish Legion who was killed in 1836. [MCA]

MACKIE, BARBARA, in Aberdeen, daughter of William Mackie in Gilcomstone, Aberdeenshire, testament, 1800, Comm. Aberdeen. [NRS]

MACKIE, JAMES, a merchant and ship-owner in Aberdeen, died in Montreal on 23 March 1833. [GNS.7.5.1833]

MACKIE, JOHN FLETCHER, born in April 1806, by 1831 he was an agent for Jersey City Rolling Mills, New Jersey, died in Saugatuck, Connecticut, in April 1851. [ANY]

MACKIE, WILLIAM, was admitted as a draff burgess of Old Aberdeen on 8 October 1808. [ACA]

MACKIE, WILLIAM, was admitted as a trade burgess of Old Aberdeen on 27 April 1823. [ACA]

MACKIE, WILLIAM, born 1816, a music seller from Aberdeen, died in Rochester, New York, on 20 July 1866. [AJ.15.8.1866]

MCKILLIGAN, MARGARET, born 1788, wife of Alexander Webster an advocate, died in Aberdeen in 1824. [AJ.24.1.1824]

MCLAGAN, CATHERINE, born 1799, widow of William Hay of Hayfield, died at 26 Constitution Street, Aberdeen, in 1846. [AJ.2.5.1846]

MCLEAN, Dr GEORGE GORDON, married Frances Helen Angus, daughter of John Angus of Tillicorthy, in Aberdeen on 6 July 1820. [SM.86.189]

MCLEAN, J. N., emigrated from Aberdeen on board the <u>Albion of Aberdeen</u> bound for Halifax, Nova Scotia, in 1836. [AJ.29.6.1836]

MCLEAN, ROBERT, a plasterer in Aberdeen, died 16 February 1844, grandfather of James Henderson McLean in Newry, Ireland. [NRS.S/H]

MCLENNAN, ALEXANDER, born 1794, a seaman in Aberdeen, was accused of housebreaking and theft in 1817. [NRS.AC17.14.40]

MCLEOD, FLORA, daughter of Donald McLeod in Schoolhill, Aberdeen, died in Toronto on 12 June 1862. [AJ.5974]

MCLEOD, JOHN, from Aberdeen, was educated at King's College, Aberdeen, in 1810, later in Honourable East India Company Service. [KCA]

MCLEOD, RODERICK, minister of St Pauls in Aberdeen, graduated Doctor of Divinity from King's College, Aberdeen, on 8 January 1793. [KCA]

MCMILLAN, WILLIAM, was admitted as a currier burgess of Old Aberdeen on 30 September 1799. [ACA]

MCNAUGHTON, MARGARET, eldest daughter of George McNaughton, late of Aberdeen, married Samuel Vial, at Hazelgrove, Illinois, on 19 November 1846. She died there on 18 May 1856. [AJ.5168; 5657]

MACPETRIE, JAMES, son of James McPetrie in Aberdeen, was educated at King's College Aberdeen, in 1815, later a surgeon in Tobago. [KCA]

MCPHERSON, Dr HUGH, born 1767, 'for 61 years a Professor in King's College, Aberdeen', died in Old Aberdeen in 1854. [AJ.12.3.1854]

MCPHERSON, HUGH, from Old Machar, graduated MA from King's College, Aberdeen, in March 1837, later a surgeon in the Service of the East India Company. [KCA]

MCPHERSON, JOHN, from Old Machar, Aberdeen, was educated at King's College, Aberdeen, in 1833, a physician in Calcutta on Honourable East India Company Service, a Member of the Royal College of Surgeons, in Old Aberdeen, graduated MD from King's College, Aberdeen, on 11 April 1845. [KCA]

MCPHERSON, NEIL, a mariner in Aberdeen, testament, 1791, Comm. Aberdeen. [NRS]

MCRAE, JOSEPH, a surgeon from Aberdeen, died in Grenada in December 1798. [EA.3688.287]

MACKRAY, PATRICK, a merchant in Demerara, son of Robert Mackray a manufacturer in Aberdeen, a deed 1824, written by his brother Robert Mackray a writer in Aberdeen. [NRS.RD5.275.8]

MCWILLIAM, JAMES, from Old Machar, Aberdeen, graduated MA from King's College, Aberdeen, in March 1835, a merchant in America. [KCA]

MAIN, JAMES, master of the <u>Ploughman of Aberdeen</u> from Aberdeen with passengers bound for Pictou, Nova Scotia, in 1812. [NRS.E504.1.24]

MAIN, JAMES, born 1819, a surgeon, arrived in Kingston, Jamaica, on 11 May 1841 on board the Rob Roy from Aberdeen. [TNA.CO140/33]

MAIN, JOHN, master of the brig Media of Aberdeen testament, 1808, Comm. Edinburgh. [NRS]

MAIR, JAMES, son of James Mair a labourer, was apprenticed to Joseph Berrie a weaver in Aberdeen from1791 to 1796. [ACA]

MAIR, JAMES, born 1832, from Savoch, died at Lake Shetek, Wisconsin, on 4 February 1875. [AJ.17.3.1875]

MAIR, JOHN, born 7 March 1798, son of George Mair and his wife Carolina Stewart in Aberdeen, was educated at King's College, Aberdeen, from 1811 to 1815, graduated MA, a physician and author in Canada. [KCA]

MAIR, JOHN, born 1822, from Aberdeen, Superintendent Carpenter of the Pacific Steam Navigation Company, died in Paita, Peru, on 24 February 1861. [AJ.5910]

MAIR, THOMAS, in Canada West, brother and heir of James Mair an advocate in Aberdeen, 1848. [NRS.S/H]

MAITLAND, JAMES, from Aberdeen, married Elizabeth Bousie from Germany, in Halifax, Nova Scotia, on 21 November 1833. [AR.30.11.1833]

MAITLAND, JANET, relict of William Milne a weaver in Aberdeen, testament, 1790, Comm. Aberdeen. [NRS]

MALCOLM, DAVID, born 1823, son of Reverend William Malcolm, died in Aberdeen in 1839. [AJ.23.10.1839]

MALCOLM, HELEN, eldest daughter of Thomas Malcolm a builder in Aberdeen, wife of Donald McBean a ship's carpenter, died in Launceston, Tasmania, Australia, on 24 August 1864. [AJ.6099]

MALCOLM, JOHN, born 1827, son of Reverend William Malcolm, died in Aberdeen in 1839. [AJ.15.11.1839]

MANN, ALEXANDER, from Aberdeen, was educated at King's College, in 1819, later a minister in Pakenham, Canada. [KCA]

MANSON, MARGARET DIANA, daughter of Alexander Manson of Oakhill, wife of George Elmslie a merchant, died at 185 King Street, Aberdeen, in 1850. [AJ.11.11.1850]

MARR, ALEXANDER, born 1736, a shipbuilder in Aberdeen, died in 1830. [AJ.7.2.1830]

MARR, WILLIAM, son of Alexander Marr a butcher in Aberdeen, was apprenticed to William Farquharson, a saddler in Aberdeen, from 1778 to 1785. [ACA]

MARSH, JAMES, master of the Caroline of Aberdeen, from Aberdeen with passengers bound for Quebec in 1854. [AH]

MARTIN, ALEXANDER, master of the Monarch of Aberdeen, from Aberdeen to St John, New Brunswick, on 20 March 1820. [NRS.E504.1.28]

MARTIN, GEORGE, was admitted as a merchant burgess of Old Aberdeen on 14 November 1799. [ACA]

MARTIN, JOHN, master of the Taurus of Aberdeen from Aberdeen with 134 passengers bound for Quebec in 1842. [BPP.1842]

MARTIN, WILLIAM, a butcher in Aberdeen, testament, 1797, Comm. Aberdeen. [NRS]

MASON, PETER, was admitted as a weaver burgess of Old Aberdeen on 9 November 1802. [ACA]

MASSIE, ALEXANDER, was admitted as a burgess of Old Aberdeen on 8 October 1808. [ACA]

MASSIE, JAMES, son of Robert Massie, a maltster in Aberdeen, was apprenticed to John Ross, a baker in Aberdeen, from 1785 to 1790. [ACA]

MASSIE, JAMES, was admitted as a farmer burgess of Old Aberdeen on 29 October 1821. [ACA]

MASSIE, JOHN, was admitted as a burgess of Old Aberdeen on 14 November 1835. [ACA]

MASSIE, WILLIAM, was admitted as a burgess of Old Aberdeen on 8 October 1808. [ACA]

MASSON, ALEXANDER, was admitted as a merchant burgess of Old Aberdeen on 27 August 1823. [ACA]

MASSON, ANN, in Aberdeen, relict of James Brebner a merchant in Aberdeen, testament, 1792, Comm. Aberdeen. [NRS]

MASSON, PETER, was admitted as a merchant burgess of Old Aberdeen on 30 October 1814. [ACA]

MASSON, WILLIAM, was admitted as a blacksmith burgess of Old Aberdeen on 18 May 1801. [ACA]

MATHEW, ROBERT, born 1804, manager of the Aberdeen Steam Navigation Company, died in Aberdeen in 1851. [AJ.2.10.1851]

MATTHEW, WILLIAM, son of William Matthew in Aberdeen, was educated at Marischal College in 1849, later a minister in Australia. [MCA]

MATHIESON, ALEXANDER, son of William Mathieson a woolcomber, was apprenticed to George Adam a shoemaker in Aberdeen, from 1786 to 1791. [ACA]

MATHIESON, CHARLES, was admitted as a burgess of Old Aberdeen on 29 September 1856. [ACA]

MATHIESON, JOHN, was admitted as a trade burgess of Old Aberdeen on 23 November 1866. [ACA]

MAVOR, MARGARET, in Aberdeen, testament, 1795, Comm. Aberdeen. [NRS]

MAXWELL, ELIZABETH, widow of Alexander Dun the Rector of Aberdeen Grammar School, died in Edinburgh in 1828. [AJ.11.9.1828]

MEARNS, ANDREW, born around 1800 in Aberdeen, a merchant in Savanna, Georgia, died on 24 February 1820. [Colonial Museum and Savanna Advertiser, 25 February 1820]

MEARNS, Dr DUNCAN, born 1779, Professor of Divinity and one of His Majesty's Chaplains for Scotland, died at King's College, Aberdeen, in 1852. [AJ.2.3.1852]

MEARNS, JOHN, from Strachan, of H.M. 6th Regiment at Colbath, Bombay, India, died in 1829, an inventory, 1834, Comm. Edinburgh, 1834. [NRS]

MEDERS, JOHN, in Aberdeen, testament, 1797, Comm. Aberdeen. [NRS]

MEFF, WILLIAM, was admitted as a trade burgess of Old Aberdeen on 27 August 1823. [ACA]

MEFFEN, ALEXANDER, was admitted as a weaver burgess of Old Aberdeen on 29 October 1821. [ACA]

MELLIS, PETER, of Old Aberdeen brewery, was admitted as a clerk burgess of Old Aberdeen on 25 October 1851. [ACA]

MELVILLE, THOMAS, son of William Melville, a merchant in Aberdeen, was educated at Marischal College in 1846, later an iron merchant in Aberdeen. [MCA]

MELVIN, ALEXANDER, was admitted as a merchant burgess of Old Aberdeen on 27 April 1807. [ACA]

MELVIN, JAMES, was admitted as a wright burgess of Old Aberdeen on 9 November 1802. [ACA]

MELVIN, JAMES, was admitted as a merchant burgess of Old Aberdeen on 30 September 1805. [ACA]

MELVIN, JOHN, was admitted as a weaver burgess of Old Aberdeen on 22 April 1799. [ACA]

MELVIN, JOHN, born 1801, a seaman in Aberdeen, was accused of housebreaking and theft in 1817. [NRS.AC17.14.40]

MELVIN, JOHN, was admitted as a burgess of Old Aberdeen on 1 October 1810. [ACA]

MELVIN, ROBERT, late merchant on Broad Street, Aberdeen, died in Boharm, Nicol township, Upper Canada, on 26 November 1835. [AJ.4591]

MELVIN, THOMAS, second son of John Melvin a weaver, was admitted as a weaver burgess of Old Aberdeen on 25 October 1813. [ACA]

MEMESS, SARAH ANN, widow of Reverend James Watt, a master of Aberdeen Grammar School, died at Berryden Cottage, Aberdeen, in 1849. [AJ.6.4.1849]

MENNIE, JOHN, son of Alexander Mennie, a merchant in Aberdeen, was educated at Marischal College in 1842, later a minister. [MCA]

MENNIE, ROBERT, a burgess of Old Aberdeen, testament, 1797, Comm. Aberdeen. [NRS]

MENZIES, JOHN, in Aberdeen, testament, 1794, Comm. Aberdeen. [NRS]

MERCHANT, WILLIAM COPLAND, born 1821, son of Richard Merchant, [1771-1822], and his wife Elizabeth Wilson, [died 1854], an engineer who died in Tobago on 5 September 1862. [St Nicholas gravestone, Aberdeen]

MESTON, THOMAS, a teacher in Aberdeen, brother of Reverend William Meston in Lille, France, 1851. [NRS.S/H]

METCALFE, WILLIAM, a traveller in Waterloo, Canada West, brother and heir of Penelope Metcalfe in Aberdeen who died on 8 February 1862. [NRS.S/H]

MICHIE, CHARLES, son of George Michie in Aberdeen, was educated at Marischal College in 1845, later a librarian at the University of Aberdeen. [MCA]

MICHIE, JOHN, from Aberdeen, a merchant in London, Canada West, died at his brother's house in Toronto on 26 September 1851. [AJ.5414]

MIDDLETON, CATHERINE, from Aberdeen, eldest daughter of James Middleton a music teacher in Meadowbank, Bon Accord, Upper Canada, married John Davidson in Woodburn, Bon Accord township, Upper Canada, on 1 November 1838. [AJ.4744]

MIDDLETON, JANET, daughter of William Middleton of Shiels a merchant in Aberdeen, testament, 1799, Comm. Aberdeen. [NRS]

MIDDLETON, JOHN, a merchant in Aberdeen, testament, 1790, Comm. Aberdeen. [NRS]

MIDDLETON, JOHN, born 1823, fourth son of Mr Middleton from Aberdeen, died in Meadowbank, Nichol township, Upper Canada, on 4 January 1841; Mrs Middleton died on 6 February 1841. [AJ.4869]

MIDDLETON, WILLIAM G., son of James Middleton a music teacher in Aberdeen, was educated at Marischal College in 1830s, later a surgeon in America. [MCA]

MILLEN, JOHN, born in Aberdeen, settled in Savanna, Georgia, in 1783, died on 28 October 1811. [Savanna Republican, 29 October 1811]

MILLER, CHARLES, sometime a cutler in London, later inAberdeen, testament, 1790, Comm. Aberdeen. [NRS]

MILLER, JOHN, a road contractor in Aberdeen, testament, 1798, Comm. Aberdeen. [NRS]

MILLER, SAMUEL, in Charleston, South Carolina, a benefactor of King's College, Aberdeen, 6 October 1794. [KCA]

MILLS, GEORGE, son of Peter Mills, a mariner in Aberdeen, graduated MA from Marischal College, later a minister. [MCA]

MILNE, ALEXANDER, a shipmaster in Aberdeen, testament, 1795, Comm. Aberdeen. [NRS]

MILNE, ALEXANDER, son of Alexander Milne, an innkeeper in Aberdeen, was educated at Marischal College in 1849. [MCA]

MILNE, ANDREW, son of John Milne at Bridge of Don, was apprenticed to Nathaniel Burnett, a baker in Aberdeen, from 1788 to 1794. [ACA]

MILNE, DAVID, was admitted as a merchant burgess of Old Aberdeen on 8 October 1808. [ACA]

MILNE, DAVID, born 26 December 1787 in Aberdeen, son of James Milne and his wife Agnes Copeland, educated a Aberdeen Grammar School and at King's College, Aberdeen, emigrated to Cincinatti, Ohio, in 1827, a merchant in Philadelphia, Pennsylvania, from 1829, died there on 30 July 1873. [AP]

MILNE, GEORGE, was admitted as a shoemaker burgess of Old Aberdeen on 1 October 1810. [ACA]

MILNE, HENRY, from Aberdeen, an Ensign of the 102nd Regiment of Foot, died in Portugal in 1796. [Anglican Church Records, Lisbon]

MILNE, HUGH, was admitted as a merchant burgess of Old Aberdeen on 24 December 1798. [ACA]

MILNE, JAMES, was educated at Marischal College in 1807, emigrated to Nova Scotia in 1815, an Episcopalian minister and educationalist, died in Fredericton, New Brunswick, on 27 March 1823. [ANQ]

MILNE, JAMES, born 1760, Provost of Aberdeen, died there in 1841. [AJ.4.10.1841]

MILNE, JAMES, was admitted as a painter burgess of Old Aberdeen on 28 October 1833. [ACA]

MILNE, JAMES, born 10 October 1810 in Aberdeen, son of James Milne and his wife Agnes Copeland, a merchant in Cincinatti, Ohio, and in Philadelphia, Pennsylvania, died in Philadelphia on 9 December 1865. [AP]

MILNE, JAMES, in Aberdeen, graduated MD from King's College, Aberdeen, on 10 April 1845. [KCA]

MILNE, JOHN, a merchant in Aberdeen, testament, 1800, Comm. Aberdeen. [NRS]

MILNE, Dr JOHN, in Bombay, India, a benefactor of King's College, Aberdeen, in December 1808. [KCA]

MILNE, JOHN, born 1812, arrived in Kingston, Jamaica, on 11 May 1841 on board the Rob Roy from Aberdeen. [TNA.CO140/33]

MILNE, JOHN, jr., was admitted as a burgess of Old Aberdeen on 8 October 1808. [ACA]

MILNE, JOHN, was admitted as a merchant burgess of Old Aberdeen on 8 October 1808. [ACA]

MILNE, JOHN, was admitted as a trade burgess of Old Aberdeen on 30 October 1820. [ACA]

MILNE, JOHN, was admitted as a baker burgess of Old Aberdeen on 27 October 1855. [ACA]

MILNE, JOHN FORSYTH, son of John Milne in Aberdeen, graduated MA from Marischal College in 1847. [MCA]

MILNE, JOSEPH, was admitted as a trade burgess of Old Aberdeen on 22 December 1823. [ACA]

MILNE, LILLIAS, wife of Reverend J. Longmuir of the Free Mariners Church, died at 16 Silver Street, Aberdeen, in 1854. [AJ.1.12.1854]

MILNE, PATRICK, of Crimondgate, died in Aberdeen on 16 May 1820. [SM.96.86]

MILNE, PETER, skipper of the Charles Forbes of Aberdeen, testament, 1819, Comm. Edinburgh. [NRS]

MILNE, ROBERT, son of Robert Milne, a shipmaster in Aberdeen, was apprenticed to George Sim, a saddler and harness-maker in Aberdeen from 1791 to 1796. [ACA]

MILNE, WILLIAM, son of George Milne, a shoemaker in Aberdeen, was apprenticed to Alexander Jopp, a cooper in Aberdeen, from 1787 to 1792. [NRS]

MILNE, WILLIAM, son of William Milne, a gardener in Old Machar, was educated at Marischal College in 1845. [MCA]

MILNE, WILLIAM, son of William Milne, a merchant in Aberdeen, graduated MA from Marischal College in 1848, later a minister. [MCA]

MINTO, ANDREW, born 1786, son of Alexander Minto a farmer in Kinnore, Huntly, a merchant in Leghorn, Italy, for thirty years, died there on 19 January 1838. [AJ.4717]

MITCHELL, ALEXANDER, was admitted as a trade burgess of Old Aberdeen in October 1816. [ACA]

MITCHELL, ALEXANDER, cashier of the Aberdeen Town and County Bank, died in Dundee in 1834. [AJ.30.10.1834]

MITCHELL, ALEXANDER, son of James Mitchell, a merchant in Aberdeen, was educated at Marischal College in 1844. [MCA]

MITCHELL, ALEXANDER, son of James Mitchell, an articifier in Aberdeen, was educated at Marischal College, graduated MA in 1846. [MCA]

MITCHELL, ALEXANDER SMITH, son of John Mitchell, an architect in Aberdeen, was educated at Marischal College, graduated MA in 1846. [MCA]

MITCHELL, CHARLES, in Cincinatti, Ohio, son and heir of Robert Mitchell a shipowner in Aberdeen, who died on 9 February 1862, [NRS.S/H]; he died in Cincinatti on 25 June 1864. [AJ.20.7.1864]

MITCHELL, DAVID, born 1732 in Old Aberdeen, educated at Marischal College, Aberdeen, died at Holloway Down, Essex, in 1803. [AJ.15.3.1803]

MITCHELL, GEORGE, son of Joseph Mitchell, a vintner in Aberdeen, was apprenticed to William Littlejohn, a wright in Aberdeen, from 1792 to 1797. [ACA]

MITCHELL, JAMES, son of James Mitchell in Aberdeen, graduated MA from Marischal College in 1816, later minister of the Scots Church in Poonah, India. [MCA]

MITCHELL, JEAN, born 1770, widow of Provost James Milne, died at 65 Gallowgate, Aberdeen, in 1853. [AJ.17.5.1853]

MITCHELL, JOHN, son of Joseph Mitchell, a vintner in Aberdeen, was apprenticed to Alexander Leslie and Company, druggists in Aberdeen, from 1787 to 1792. [ACA]

MITCHELL, JOHN, born 1785 in Aberdeen, died in Halifax, Nova Scotia, on 25 January 1831. [AR.29.1.1831]

MITCHELL, JOHN, was admitted as a weaver burgess of Old Aberdeen on 23 December 1854. [ACA]

MITCHELL, MARGARET ANN, widow of John Robert Smith of Concraig, died in Aberdeen in 1834. [AJ.6.6.1834]

MITCHELL, PETER, was admitted as a weaver burgess of Old Aberdeen on 12 November 1804. [ACA]

MITCHELL, PETER, was admitted as a merchant burgess of Old Aberdeen on 29 September 1806. [ACA]

MITCHELL, Mrs SUSAN, wife of John Mitchell a merchant in Virginia, sister and her of John Strachan in Aberdeen in 1797. [NRS.S/H]

MITCHELL, WILLIAM, was admitted as a weaver burgess of Old Aberdeen on 26 October 1818. [ACA]

MOIR, ALEXANDER, born 1767, a hosier, died at 103 Gallowgate, Aberdeen, in 1851. [AJ.10.11.1851]

MOIR, Dr ALEXANDER, in St Croix, Danish West Indies, a benefactor of King's College, Aberdeen, 15 February 1783. [KCA]

MOIR, JAMES, born 1723, died in Aberdeen in 1824. 'He was the brother-in-law of the veteran McDougal who supported General Wolfe after he received his mortal wound on the Plain of Quebec'. [AJ.7.3.1824]

MOIR, JAMES, from Aberdeen, was educated at Marischal College in 1849, later a minister. [MCA]

MOIR, Reverend J. S., born 1823 in Aberdeen, was Principal of Corporate High School, Sandhurst, Australia, died on 7 August 1876. [AJ.6721]

MOIR, JAMES, jr., born 1849 in Aberdeen, son of James Moir an insurance agent, died in the USA on 3 May 1875. [AJ.2.6.1875]

MOIR, PATRICK, son of Dr James Moir in Aberdeen, married Maria White, eldest daughter of John White, in Quebec on 19 June 1838. [AJ.4724]

MOIR, ROBERT, a merchant in Aberdeen, testament, 1798, Comm. Aberdeen. [NRS]

MOIR, WILLIAM, in Aberdeen, late in Brazil, 2 June 1821. [NRS.RGS.163.54]

MOIR, WILLIAM, born 1826 in Aberdeen, emigrated to USA in 1835, a watchmaker who died in New York on 21 March 1896. [ANY]

MORE, AGNES, born 1762, died at 66 Schoolhill, Aberdeen, in 1842. [AJ.9.9.1842]

MORE, GEORGE, of Raeden, born 1751, died in Aberdeen in 1828. [AJ.14.3.1828]

MORE, GEORGE, son of Provost George More of Aberdeen, a Major of the 24th Bombay Native Infantry, died at Asseerghur, India, in 1843. [AJ.10.11.1843]

MORE, GILBERT, second son of Alexander More, the Customs Collector in Aberdeen, died in Havannah, Cuba, on 15 April 1821. [S.231.200]

MORGAN, JOHN, master of the Harmony of Aberdeen, trading between Pictou, Nova Scotia, and Dundee in 1819. [NRS.E504.11.21]

MORGAN, Dr WILLIAM, late Rector of Kingston, Jamaica, later Professor of Philosophy in Marischal College, Aberdeen, testament, 1789, Comm. Aberdeen. [NRS]

MORICE, ARTHUR, son of Robert Morice an advocate in Aberdeen, was educated at Marischal College in 1841, later in Natal, South Africa. [MCA]

MORICE, GEORGE, son of Robert Morice an advocate in Aberdeen, a student at Marischal College in 1830s, later a merchant in Ceylon. [MCA]

MORICE, ISOBEL, relict of John Monfond a shipmaster in Aberdeen, testament, 1792, Comm. Aberdeen. [NRS]

MORICE, JAMES, master of the Fairfield of Aberdeen from Aberdeen with passengers bound for Quebec in 1820. [QC]

MORICE, RACHEL, born 1741, widow of David Morice an advocate and Sheriff Substitute for Aberdeenshire, died in Aberdeen in 1825. [AJ.19.12.1825] [SM.97.128]

MORICE, ROBERT, born 1775, a writer in Edinburgh, son of David Morice an advocate in Aberdeen, was admitted as a Notary Public on 16 June 1792, died in 1834. [AJ.29.3.1834] [NRS.NP2.34.351]

MORREN, HUGH, born 1796, a merchant, died in Aberdeen in 1832. [AJ.13.8.1832]

MORISON, ALEXANDER, son of John Morison, a wright in Aberdeen, was apprenticed to Joseph Yule, a tailor in Aberdeen, from 1787 to 1793. [ACA]

MORISON, ALEXANDER, son of John Morison in Aberdeen, was educated at Marischal College in 1841. [MCA]

MORISON, HELEN, daughter of James Morison of Elsick, died in Aberdeen in 1840. [AJ.2.11.1840]

MORRISON, JAMES, master of the Centurion of Aberdeen from Aberdeen, with passengers bound for Halifax, Nova Scotia, in 1811;

master of the Mary of Aberdeen from Aberdeen with passengers bound for Halifax, Nova Scotia, in 1811 and 1812. [NRS.E504.1.24]; master of the Pacific of Aberdeen from Aberdeen with passengers bound for Quebec in 1835. [QM]

MORRISON, JAMES, son of James Morrison a mariner in Aberdeen, was educated at Marischal College in 1847, later a commercial agent in Aberdeen. [MCA]

MORRISON, JAMES, born 1835, only son of George Morrison, a shipmaster on Aberdeen, died in Melbourne, Victoria, Australia, on 13 February 1862. [AJ.5964]

MORRISON, JEAN, spouse of Dr Robert Hamilton, Professor of Mathematics at Marischal College, died in 1825. [AJ.8.2.1825]

MORRISON, J., master of the Pacific of Aberdeen from Aberdeen with passengers bound for Quebec in 1835. [QM]

MORRISON, JOHN, son of John Morrison in Aberdeen, was educated at Marischal College in 1828, later was town clerk of Sydney, New South Wales, Australia. [MCA]

MORISON, WALTER CHALMERS, son of James Morison a gentleman in Aberdeen, was educated at Marischal College in 1840. [MCA]

MORRISON, WILLIAM, eldest son of John Morrison the factor of Craigievar, a baker in Aberdeen later in Port Morant, Jamaica, by 1799. [NRS.CS26.909.29]

MORRISON, WILLIAM, born 1817, arrived in Kingston, Jamaica, on 11 May 1841 on board the Rob Roy from Aberdeen. [TNA.CO140/33]

MORISON, WILLIAM, born 1824, third son of Captain John Morison master of the Pacific of Aberdeen, died in Quebec on 4 June 1842. [AJ.4930]

MORRISON, WILLIAM, born 1783, from Demerara, died in Aberdeen on 5 February 1859. [CM.21.647]

MORTIMER, DAVID, emigrated from Aberdeen to Australia in 1852, settled at Gemmell's Station, Wooragay, South Australia, in 1856. [AJ.5663]

MORTIMER, JOHN, son of George Mortimer, a stabler in Aberdeen, was apprenticed to John Ross, a baker in Aberdeen, from 1789 to 1793. [ACA]

MORTIMER, JOHN T., son of Alexander Mortimer a baker in Aberdeen, was educated at Marischal College in 1835, later a Customs officer in Melbourne, Victoria, Australia. [MCA]

MORTIMER, WILLIAM, born in February 1799, son of John Mortimer, a fisherman in Aberdeen, and his wife Jean Anderson, was educated a King's College, Aberdeen, from 1812 to 1816, later a merchant in Pictou, Nova Scotia. [KCA]

MORTIMER, WILLIAM, son of James Mortimer a merchant in Aberdeen, graduated MA from Marischal College in 1849, later a licentiate. [MCA]

MORTIMER, WILLIAM, MD, late of the Honourable East India Company Service in Madras, India, died at 118 Crown Street, Aberdeen, in 1848. [AJ.16.5.1848]

MOWAT, CHARLES EGGLESTONE, son of James Mowat a merchant in Aberdeen, died on Tobago on 27 February 1836. [AJ.27.4.1836]

MOWAT, JAMES, third son of James Mowat a merchant in Aberdeen, died in Demerara on 21 January 1838. [AJ.4710]; testament, 1848. [NRS]

MOWAT, ROBERT, born 1790 in Aberdeen, died 28 October 1867 in New Brunswick. [Anglican cemetery, East St John, NB]

MOSMAN, Mrs, widow of Thomas Mosman of Middlefield, an advocate in Aberdeen, died in 1804. [AJ.11.12.1804]

MUIL, JOHN, son of John Muil a minister in Aberdeen, was educated at Marischal College in 1849, an advocacate in Aberdeen by 1858. [MCA]

MUIR, GEORGE FALCONER, son of Alexander Muir an advocate in Aberdeen, was educated at Marischal College in 1848, later a writer. [MCA]

MUNN, Captain, master of the Jane Boyd of Aberdeen from Aberdeen bound for Quebec in 1855. [QM]

MUNRO, JOHN, born 1788, a straw hat manufacturer, died in Queen Street, Aberdeen, in 1840. [AJ.30.7.1840]

MURRAY, ALEXANDER, DD, formerly in London, later in Philadelphia, Pennsylvania, a benefactor of King's College, Aberdeen, 6 September 1793. [KCA]

MURRAY, ALEXANDER, born 1799, died in Aberdeen in 1838. [AJ.10.2.1838]

MURRAY, ALEXANDER, son of George Murray in Aberdeen, graduated MA from Marischal College in 1844, later a minister. [MCA]

MURRAY, DAVID, born 1851 in Aberdeen, died in Brooklyn, New York, on 22 October 1873. [AJ.19.11.1873]

MURRAY, JAMES, a thread dyer in Aberdeen, testament, 1793, Comm. Aberdeen. [NRS]

MURRAY, JOHN, in St Kitts, British West Indies, son and heir of William Murray in Aberdeen in 1792. [NRS.S/H]

MURRAY, JOHN, a flax dresser who emigrated from Aberdeen to America before 1824, was naturalised in New York on 12 September 1840. [N.Y., Southern District Court Records]

MURRAY, JOHN, born 1812, a shoemaker, arrived in Kingston, Jamaica, on 11 May 1841 on board the Rob Roy from Aberdeen. [TNA.CO140/33]

MURRAY, WILLIAM, a merchant in Aberdeen, testament, 1792, Comm. Aberdeen. [NRS]

MURRAY, WILLIAM, clerk of the Aberdeen Lime Company, a victim of crime in 1825. [NRS.JC26.1825.29]

MURRAY, WILLIAM SIMSON, son of Alexander Murray in Aberdeen, graduated MA from Marischal College in 1844, and MB in 1850. [MCA]

MUTCH, ALEXANDER, born 1756 in Aberdeen, emigrated to Prince Edward Island in 1786, died at Mount Herbert in 1828. [Crossroads gravestone, PEI]

MUTCH, GEORGE, was admitted as a merchant burgess of Old Aberdeen on 1 October 1798. [ACA]

NAIRN, JANET, born 1760, widow of Adam Staples the Convenor of the Incorporated Trades of Aberdeen, died at 132 High Street, Old Aberdeen, in 1842. [AJ.10.4.1842]

NICOLL, ALEXANDER, at Bridge of Don, was admitted as a butcher burgess of Old Aberdeen on 10 November 1792. [ACA]

NICOL, ALEXANDER, a maltster in Aberdeen, testament, 1794, Comm. Aberdeen. [NRS]

NICOL, ALEXANDER, was admitted as a stone merchant burgess of Old Aberdeen on 3 October 1832. [ACA]

NICOL, GEORGE, emigrated from Aberdeen on the <u>Albion of Aberdeen</u> bound for Halifax, Nova Scotia, in 1836. [AJ.29.6.1836]

NICOL, JAMES, was admitted as a burgess of Old Aberdeen on 2 October 1815. [ACA]

NICOL, JAMES, was admitted as a trade burgess of Old Aberdeen on 30 October 1820. [ACA]

NICOL, JAMES, son of James Nicol an advocate in Aberdeen, was educated at Marischal College in 1840, later a writer in Oban. [MCA]

NICOL, JOHN, a merchant in Aberdeen, testament, 1794, Comm. Aberdeen. [NRS]

NICOL, JOHN, in Aberdeen, graduated MA from King's College, Aberdeen, on 28 March 1812, later a planter in Jamaica. [KCA]

NICOL, JOHN, born 1807, a merchant and shipowner, died at 20 Ship Row, Aberdeen, in 1852. [AJ.29.10.1852]

NICOL, LESLIE, was admitted as a merchant burgess of Old Aberdeen on 25 October 1839. [ACA]

NICOL, PETER, was admitted as a burgess of Old Aberdeen on 4 November 1799. [ACA]

NICOLL, THOMAS, at Bridge of Don, was admitted as a butcher burgess of Old Aberdeen on 10 November 1792. [ACA]

NICOL, THOMAS, was admitted as a trade burgess of Old Aberdeen on 30 October 1815. [ACA]

NICOLL, WILLIAM, at Bridge of Don, was admitted as a butcher burgess of Old Aberdeen on 10 November 1792. [ACA]

NICOL, WILLIAM, was admitted as a tailor burgess of Old Aberdeen on 25 February 1814. [ACA]

NICOLSON, JAMES, son of William Nicolson a merchant in Aberdeen, graduated MA from Marischal College in 1849, later Dean of Brechin. [MCA]

NISBET, MARGARET, widow of Reverend David Waddel, died at her son's house in Chapel Street, Aberdeen, in 1831. [AJ.25.5.1831]

NIVEN, JOHN, of Thornton, born 1743, died in Aberdeen in 1828. [AJ.11.7.1828]

NORIE, GEORGE, a skipper in Aberdeen, inventory, 1809, Comm. Aberdeen. [NRS]

OCHTERLONY, BATHIA, widow of Charles Tait the Sheriff Substitute, died in Aberdeen in 1800. [AJ.8.11.1800]

OGG, GEORGE WATSON STUART, son of Henry Ogg a merchant in Aberdeen, graduated MA from Marischal College in 1845, and MB in 1854. [MCA]

OGILVIE, ELIZABETH, widow of Patrick Anderson of Bourtrie, died in Aberdeen in 1800. [AJ.5.4.1800]

OGILVIE, ELIZABETH, born 1805, youngest daughter of Charles Bannerman, died in Aberdeen in 1814. [AJ.4.7.1814]

OGILVIE, ELIZABETH, in Aberdeen, sister and heir of James Ogilvie in America later in London, 1832. [NRS.S/H]

OGILVIE, ELIZABETH, daughter of Reverend John Ogilvie in Midmar, died at Mackie Place Cottage, Aberdeen, in 1850. [AJ.17.9.1850]

OGILVIE, HELEN, born 1745, widow of John Paterson a writer died in Aberdeen in 1809. [AJ.25.3.1809]

OGILVY, JAMES, born 1760 in Aberdeen, a teacher in Virginia and Kentucky, died in Aberdeen on 18 September 1820. [ANY]

OGILVY, JEAN, youngest daughter of Reverend Dr S. Ogilvy in Old Aberdeen, married Captain John Gordon of the Royal Artillery, son of Lieutenant Colonel Gordon of Coynachie, in Old Aberdeen on 4 September 1822. [SM.90.519]

OGILVIE, JEAN FLETCHER, in Aberdeen, sister and heir of James Ogilvie in America later in London, 1832. [NRS.S/H]

OGILVIE, JOHN CHARLES, MD, born 1785, died 1839. [AJ.19.2.1839]

OGILVIE, JOHN, son of John Ogilvie a baker in Aberdeen, graduated MA from Marischal College in 1845, MB in 1853, and MD in 1859. [MCA]

OGILVIE, MARGARET, in Aberdeen, sister and heir of James Ogilvie in America later in London, 1832. [NRS.S/H]

OGILVIE, MARGARET, daughter of Reverend John Ogilvie in Midmar, died in Aberdeen, in 1844. [AJ.10.5.1844]

OGILVIE, THEOPHILUS, of Auchlunies, born 1722, for many years the Customs Collector of Aberdeen, died in 1807. [AJ.13.4.1807]

OGILVIE, SKENE, born 1754, late minister of Old Machar, Aberdeen, died in London in 1831. [AJ.12.12.1831]

OGILVIE, WILLIAM, Professor of Humanity in King's College, Aberdeen, died there in 1819. [AJ.14.2.1819]

OGSTON, MARTHA, in Aberdeen, testament, 1791, Comm. Aberdeen. [NRS]

OLDMAN, ANDREW, born 1773, a merchant, died at Victoria Street, Aberdeen, in 1851. [AJ.10.7.1851]

OSWALD, Mrs AGNES, born 1788, eldest daughter of Reverend Dr Kidd, widow of Captain James Oswald, died at 100 Chapel Street, Aberdeen, in 1847. [AJ.19.3.1847]

OSWALD, HENRY, son of James Oswald a mariner in Aberdeen, was educated at Marischal College in 1840, later a shipbroker and a baillie of Aberdeen. [MCA]

OSWALD, Captain JAMES, master of the brig Aberdeenshire, died in Halifax, Nova Scotia, on 24 October 1832, [AR.10.11.1832]

PALMER, JOHN, born 1798, an apprentice from Aberdeen, was drowned in the wreck of the whaling ship Oscar of Aberdeen in 1813. [AJ]

PARK, ERNEST GORDON, born in Aberdeen, a carpenter who emigrate to USA in 1842, settled in Union District, South Carolina, was naturalised there on 9 October 1849. [NARA]

PATERSON, HENRY, manager of the North of Scotland Banking Company in Aberdeen in 1849. [POD]

PATERSON, Dr JOHN, son of John Paterson in Aberdeen, a planter at Baulk, Hanover parish, Jamaica, died in Jamaica during 1789.

PATERSON, JOHN, son of John Paterson in Rubislaw, Aberdeen, was educated at Marischal College, Aberdeen, from 1836 to 1840, graduated MA, a merchant in Port Elizabeth, Cape of Good Hope, South Africa. [MCA]

PATERSON, JOHN, born 1837 in Aberdeen, died in Fernando Po, an island in the Bight of Biafra, on 2 February 1863. [AJ.6061]

PATERSON, PETER, a seaman from Aberdeen, died aboard the brigantine Dove when bound from Berbice to Halifax, Nova Scotia, on 9 June 1831. [AR.2.7.1831]

PATERSON, ROBERT, a tanner in Aberdeen, testament, 1793, Comm. Aberdeen. [NRS]

PATERSON, WILLIAM, was admitted as a merchant burgess of Old Aberdeen on 29 April 1829. [ACA]

PATILLO, ALEXANDER, born 1742 in Aberdeen, died in Chester, Nova Scotia, on 31 December 1833. [HJ.13.1.1834]

PATON, MARGARET, born 1748, died in Old Aberdeen in 1838. [AJ.28.5.1838]

PAUL, ALEXANDER, was admitted as a shoemaker burgess of Old Aberdeen on 7 May 1829. [ACA]

PAUL, ANN, in Aberdeen, widow of John Hope, testament, 1790, Comm. Aberdeen. [NRS]

PAUL, ROBERT, a block-printer in Aberdeen, nephew and heir of Alexander Telfer a watchmaker in Antigua in 1806. [NRS.S/H]

PAUL, ROBERT, born 1821, with Margery Paul, born 1821, arrived in Kingston, Jamaica, on 11 May 1841 on board the Rob Roy from Aberdeen. [TNA.CO140/33]

PAUL, Mrs SUSANNA, in Aberdeen, relict of Andrew Paul, Aberdeen, testament, 1798, Comm. Aberdeen. [NRS]

PAULL, THOMAS, born 1777, son of James Paull and his wife Margaret Black, died in Trinidad on 31 December 1803. [St Nicholas gravestone, Aberdeen]

PAUL, W., was admitted as a trade burgess of Old Aberdeen on 30 October 1820. [ACA]

PAUL, WILLIAM, jr., was admitted as a gardener burgess of Old Aberdeen on 7 November 1796. [ACA]

PAUL, Reverend WILLIAM, was admitted as a burgess of Old Aberdeen in November 1811. [ACA]

PAUL, WILLIAM, Professor of Natural Philosophy in King's College, Aberdeen, died in 1834. [AJ.3.3.1834]

PEAT, JAMES, Collector of Excise in Aberdeen, testament, 1797, Comm. Aberdeen. [NRS]

PETERKIN, JAMES, born 1799, from Woodside, Aberdeen, died in Toronto on 18 March 1876. [AJ.6691]

PETRIE, JAMES, son of George Petrie, sheriff officer in Old Aberdeen, was apprenticed to James Ramsay, a tailor in Aberdeen, from 1785 to 1791. [ACA]

PHILIP, ALEXANDER, son of William Philip a merchant in Aberdeen, was educated at Marischal College in 1840. [MCA]

PHILIP, JOHN ROY, son of William Philip a merchant in Aberdeen, was educated at Marischal College in 1841. [MCA]

PHILIP, MARGARET, from Aberdeen, married James Sievewright in Stonington, Connecticut, on 22 September 1847. [AJ.5208]

PHILIP, MARGARET MENZIES, eldest daughter of William Philip late of Aberdeen, died in New Aberdeen, Canada West, on 30 July 1849. [AJ.5303]

PHILIP, Captain WILLIAM, born 1775, 'the oldest shipmaster in Aberdeen, died on 27 March 1849. [ACA]

PHILLIPS, ANDREW, son of Andrew Phillips a merchant in Aberdeen, was educated at Marischal College in 1840, later schoolmaster of Glen Muick. [MCA]

PHILLIPS, ANN, born 1790, wife of Robert Mitchell, manager of the Aberdeen, Leith, and Clyde Shipping Company, died in Aberdeen in 1849. [AJ.5.2.1849]

PHILIPS, NEIL SMITH, born 1823, eldest son of Andrew Philips in Union Row, Aberdeen, died in Demerara on13 December 1842. [AJ.4960]

PIRIE, ANDREW, son of Alexander Pirie, a wheelwright in Aberdeen, was apprenticed to James Finnie, a wright in Aberdeen, from 1789 to 1794. [ACA]

PIRIE, ANDREW, born 1797 in Aberdeen, died in St Paul's, Antigua, on 22 June 1871. [AJ.2.8.1871]

PIRIE, ANNE, widow of George Kerr a physician in Aberdeen, died there in 1844. [AJ.6.6.1844]

PIRIE, GEORGE, in Canada, brother and heir of Thomas Pirie, son of George Pirie a merchant in Aberdeen, 1841. [NRS.S/H]

PIRIE, GEORGE, son of Professor William Pirie in Aberdeen, was educated at Marischal College in 1850s, later a Captain of the Madras Army in India. [MCA]

PIRIE, JAMES, master of the Cambria of Aberdeen from Aberdeen with passengers bound for Halifax, Nova Scotia, and Quebec in 1812. [NRS.E504.1.24]; master of the Morningfield of Aberdeen, from Stornaway with passengers bound for Quebec on 5 August 1815. [NRS.E504.33.3]

PIRIE, JAMES, in Trinidad, son and heir to his parents, Ann Donaldson and her husband John Pirie a merchant in Aberdeen in 1813. [NRS.S/H]

PIRIE, JAMES, son of James Pirie an inspector in Aberdeen, graduated MA from Marischal College in 1841, later a minister. [MCA]

PIRIE, JAMES, late goldsmith and jeweller in Aberdeen, died in Guernsey, Channel Islands, in 1849. [AJ.21.9.1849]

PIRIE, PATRICK, a merchant in Aberdeen, testament, 1793, Comm. Aberdeen. [NRS]

PIRIE, THOMAS, born 1803 in Aberdeen, son of George Pirie a merchant, died in Mandal, Norway, on 19 June 1839. [AJ.4774]

PIRIE, WILLIAM, a merchant in Aberdeen, married Mary Hay White, only daughter of David White of Montego Bay, Jamaica, at Lowerbanks on 27 July 1811. [SM.73.553]

PIRIE, WILLIAM, born 1783, a manufacturer in Aberdeen, died at Cotton Lodge in 1835. [AJ.20.7.1835]

PITTENDREIGH, JOHN, the younger, a merchant in Aberdeen, a letter, 1813. [NRS.CH12.30.105]

PLEDGE, EBENEZER, son of a Baptist minister in Aberdeen, graduated MA from Marischal College in 1840. [MCA]

POLSON, GRACE, second daughter of Hugh Polson a merchant in Aberdeen, married Robert McLeod a saddler from Ross-shire, in Montreal, Quebec, on 19 May 1834. [AJ.4507]

POLSON, HENRY, from Old Machar, was educated at King's College in 1848, later a surgeon in the British Army. [KCA]

POLSON, HENRY, was admitted as a burgess of Old Aberdeen on 25 October 1851. [ACA]

POLSON, JOHN, was admitted as a burgess of Old Aberdeen on 7 November 1796. [ACA]

POLSON, JOHN, jr., was admitted as a burgess of Old Aberdeen on 29 October 1828. [ACA]

POLSON, PATRICK, was admitted as a burgess of Old Aberdeen on 25 October 1851. [ACA]

POLSON, ROBERT LESLIE, in Old Aberdeen, graduated MD from King's College, Aberdeen, on 26 July 1847. [KCA]

POLSON, SARAH, only daughter of John Polson in Old Aberdeen, married D. Melville a merchant in Berbice, in Old Aberdeen on 31 January 1828. [S.846, 114]

POPPLEWELL, JOHN, late a manufacturer in Aberdeen, died in New York on 16 September 1845. [AJ.5103]

PORTER, HUGH, a merchant in Aberdeen, an equestration, in 1826. [SM.97.253]

PORTER, MARJORY, in Footdee, Aberdeen, testament, 1794, Comm. Aberdeen. [NRS]

PRATT, ALEXANDER, from Aberdeen, died in Bothwell, Canada West, on 6 July 1876. [AJ.6708]

PRIMROSE, Captain GEORGE, born 1781, died in Old Aberdeen in 1842. [AJ.14.6.1842]

PRIMROSE, THOMAS, born 11 December 1808 in Aberdeen, son of Reverend William Primrose and his wife Isabella Gibb, was educated at Aberdeen Grammar School and Marischal College, an advocate in America, died in Aberdeen on 18 January 1886. [SAA]

PRIMROSE, WILLIAM, emigrated from Aberdeen on the <u>Albion of Aberdeen</u> bound for Halifax, Nova Scotia, in 1836. [AJ.29.6.1836]

PRIMROSE, WILLIAM, MD, son of Reverend William Primrose in Aberdeen, an assistant surgeon of the 44th Regiment, died at Gundamuck, Afghanistan, on 13 January 1842. [AJ.4958]

PRINGLE, HENRY, from Aberdeen, died in Savannah, Georgia, on 10 October 1867. [AJ.18.12.1867]

PROCTOR, JOHN, was admitted as a trade burgess of Old Aberdeen on 27 October 1817. [ACA]

PYPER, ALEXANDER EWING, son of James Pyper a horse hirer in Aberdeen, was educated at Marischal College in 1844, later a schoolteacher in Newburgh, Aberdeenshire. [MCA]

PYPER, JAMES, born 1840, youngest son of John Pyper, 106 King Street, Aberdeen, died in Georgetown, Demerara, on 1 September 1864. [AJ.6095]

RAE, ALEXANDER, was admitted as a trade burgess of Old Aberdeen on 2 October 1816. [ACA]

RAE, Captain DAVID M., master of the <u>Amity of Aberdeen</u> from Aberdeen bound for Quebec in 1835, 1836. [AJ]

RAE, GEORGE, was admitted as a trade burgess of Old Aberdeen on 5 October 1826. [ACA]

RAE, GEORGE, was admitted as a butcher burgess of Old Aberdeen on 25 November 1854. [ACA]

RAE, JAMES, was admitted as a weaver burgess of Old Aberdeen on 5 November 1801. [ACA]

RAE, JAMES, was admitted as a merchant burgess of Old Aberdeen on 5 November 1801. [ACA]

RAE, JOHN, born 1 June 1796 in Aberdeen, son of John Rae and his wife Margaret Cuthbert, was educated at Marischal College and at Edinburgh University, emigrated to Canada, a teacher, doctor, and economist, died on Staten Island, New York, on 14 July 1872. [WA]

RAE, JOHN, was admitted as a trade burgess of Old Aberdeen in October 1816. [ACA]

RAE, JOHN, son of Nathaniel Rae a merchant in Aberdeen, was educated at Marischal College in 1849. [MCA]

RAE, PETER, was admitted as a draff burgess of Old Aberdeen on 8 October 1808. [ACA]

RAE, WILLIAM, was admitted as a weaver burgess of Old Aberdeen on 27 October 1806. [ACA]

RAE, WILLIAM, was admitted as a trade burgess of Old Aberdeen on 27 October 1817. [ACA]

RAE, WILLIAM, master of the Augusta of Aberdeen from Aberdeen with passengers bound for Quebec in 1836. [QM]

RAE, WILLIAM, son of William Rae in Aberdeen, was educated at Marischal College from 1835 to 1839, graduated MA, later a school teacher in Buenos Ayres, Argentina, and in Monte Video, Uruguay. [MCA]

RAE, WILLIAM, son of George Rae a lawyer in Aberdeen, at Marischal College in 1841. [MCA]

RAEBURN, CATHERINE, wife of James Morice in Montreal, Quebec, heir to her grandfather Robert Marnoch a wright in Aberdeen, 1853. [NRS.S/H]

RAGG, WILLIAM B., son of David Ragg a merchant in Aberdeen, graduated MA from Marischal College in 1846. [MCA]

RAINNIE, ALEXANDER, was admitted as a trade burgess of Old Aberdeen on 27 October 1817. [ACA]

RAINNIE, ALEXANDER, a builder, died in Aberdeen in 1845. [AJ.4.4.1845]

RAINY, GEORGE, a lecturer in Aberdeen, an honorary MD of King's College, Aberdeen, on 14 April 1848. [KCA]

RAINY, JOHN, a shipmaster in Aberdeen, testament, 1800, Comm. Aberdeen. [NRS]

RAINNIE, MARTHA, youngest daughter of S. Rainnie in Aberdeen, married Captain Francis J. McAlpine of Halifax, Nova Scotia, in Miramachi, New Brunswick, on 4 November 1839. [NBC.30.11.1839]

RAINNIE, PATRICK, was admitted as a merchant burgess of Old Aberdeen on 5 November 1801. [ACA]

RAINY, ROBERT, was admitted as a burgess of Old Aberdeen on 8 October 1808. [ACA]

RAITT, ALEXANDER, of Barkmill, Aberdeen, died on St Lucia, Windward Islands, in 1817. [S.45.17]

RAITT, GEORGE, a skipper in Aberdeen, inventory, 1812, Comm. Aberdeen. [NRS]

RAMAGE, MARGARET, wife of James Rettie a jeweller in Aberdeen, died at 7 Thistle Street, Aberdeen, in 1852. [AJ.8.12.1852]

RAMSAY, ARCHIBALD, son of Samuel Ramsay, a tidesman in Aberdeen, was apprenticed to James Ramsay, a tailor in Aberdeen, from 1784 to 1790. [ACA]

RAMSAY, HENRY, in the Service of the Honourable East India Company, was wounded in a duel in China and died from the wounds in Aberdeen in July 1808. [AJ.31.7.1808]

RAMSAY, JOHN, died in Aberdeen in 1814. [AJ.15.4.1814]

RANNIE, THOMAS, born in 1771, a builder, died in Aberdeen in1834. [AJ.13.1.1834]

RATTRAY, ROBERT GORDON, in Aberdeen, graduated MD from King's College, Aberdeen, on 10 April 1845. [KCA]

RAY, WILLIAM, son of William Ray in Aberdeen, was educated at Marischal College in 1845. [MCA]

READ, WILLIAM, son of William Read a merchant in Aberdeen, settled in New South Wales before 1854. [NRS.S/H.1854]

REID, ADAM, born 1795 in Aberdeen, died on Mount Desire, Carriacou by Grenada, on 21 February 1867. [S.7395]

REID, ALEXANDER, a flaxdresser in Aberdeen, testament, 1799, Comm. Aberdeen. [NRS]

REID, ALEXANDER, son of William Reid a writer in Aberdeen, was educated at Marischal College in 1844. [MCA]

REID, GEORGE, born 1813, a druggist, died in Crown Court, Union Street, Aberdeen, in 1849. [AJ.19.8.1849]

REID, JAMES, formerly in Wauchandale of Echt, Aberdeenshire, later in Aberdeen, testament, 1793, Comm. Aberdeen. [NRS]

REID, JAMES RICHARD, MA, born 1811, parish schoolmaster in Footdee, Aberdeen, died at 6 Forbes Street, Aberdeen, in 1846. [AJ.4.4.1846]

REID, JANET, in Aberdeen, was accused of murder in 1817. [NRS.AD14.17.55]

REID, JEAN, widow of Lachlan McKinnon a shipmaster in Aberdeen, died in 1846. [AJ.9.6.1846]

REID, Reverend JOHN, born 1739, a Roman Catholic priest, died in Aberdeen in 1816. [AJ.24.1.1816]

REID, MARGARET, born 1752, wife of Reverend Dr John Ogilvie in Midmar, died in Aberdeen in 1804. [AJ.18.9.1804]

REID, PETER, son of Peter Reid a coachman in Aberdeen, at Marischal College in 1850s, later a chemist in Wiesbaden, Germany. [MCA]

REITH, ROBERT, son of John Reith, a tailor in Aberdeen, was apprenticed to William Dunn, a merchant in Aberdeen, from 1786 to 1791. [ACA]

REID, ROBERT, from Aberdeen, was educated at King's College in 1846. [KCA]

REID, THOMAS BISSET, son of Thomas Reid a merchant in Aberdeen, was educated at Marischal College in 1849 [MCA]

REID, WILLIAM L., from Aberdeen, was educated at King's College in 1841, later an advocate in Aberdeen. [KCA]

REID, WILLIAM, master of the Margaret of Aberdeen from Leith with passengers bound for Port Adelaide, South Australia, in October 1852. [LCL.4138]

RENNY, JAMES, was admitted as a draff burgess of Old Aberdeen on 8 October 1808. [ACA]

RETTIE, MIDDLETON, born 1768, died in 26 Broad Street, Aberdeen, in 1853. [AJ.12.5.1853]

RETTIE, MIDDLETON, son of William Rettie a merchant in Aberdeen, was educated at Marischal College in 1843, later an advocate in Edinburgh. [MCA]

RHIND, CHARLES, from Aberdeen, emigrated to America before 1810, a merchant and diplomat. [WA]

RIACH, JAMES, was admitted as a weaver burgess of Old Aberdeen on 22 April 1799. [ACA]

RIACH, WILLIAM LYON, son of John Riach in Aberdeen, was educated at Marischal College in 1842, later a minister. [MCA]

RICHARDSON, JOHN, a manufacturer in Aberdeen, died in 1840. [AJ.25.6.1840]

RIDDELL, DAVID, son of William Riddell, a cobbler in Aberdeen, was apprenticed to George Strachan, a shoemaker in Aberdeen, from 1785 to 1790. [ACA]

RIDDEL, DONALDSON, son of John Riddel at Windmill Brae, Aberdeen, was apprenticed to George Beet, a blacksmith in Aberdeen, from 1789 to 1794. [ACA]

RIDDEL, WILLIAM, son of James Riddel in Aberdeen, was educated at Marischal College in 1840. [MCA]

RIDDLER, JOHN JAMIESON, in Illinois, son and heir of John Riddler a gardener in Aberdeen who died on 25 November 1843. [NRS.S/H]

RITCHIE, ALEXANDER, master of the brigantine Ann of Aberdeen, inventory, 1820, Comm. Aberdeen. [NRS]

RITCHIE, HECTOR, formerly in Old Overtoun, later in Old Aberdeen, testament, 1792, Comm. Aberdeen. [NRS]

RITCHIE, WILLIAM, born 1737, a former baillie of Aberdeen, died there in 1814. [AJ.8.4.1814]

ROBB, ALEXANDER, from Old Machar, Aberdeen, was educated at King's College, Aberdeen, in 1848, a minister in Jamaica. [KCA]

ROBB, GEORGE, son of James Robb a carpenter in Aberdeen, was educated at Marischal College in 1840, later a merchant in Aberdeen. [MCA]

ROBB, JAMES, was admitted as a trade burgess of Old Aberdeen in October 1816. [ACA]

ROBB, JAMES, was admitted as a merchant burgess of Old Aberdeen on 25 October 1824. [ACA]

ROBB, JOHN, was admitted as a burgess of Old Aberdeen on 8 October 1808. [ACA]

ROB, JOHN, a mariner in Aberdeen, inventory, 1817, Comm. Aberdeen. [NRS]

ROBB, PETER, was admitted as a merchant burgess of Old Aberdeen on 29 October 1804. [ACA]

ROBB, PETER, was admitted as a merchant burgess of Old Aberdeen on 8 October 1808. [ACA]

ROBB, WILLIAM, a mail guard of Park Street, Aberdeen, was accused of breach of trust and theft at Ellon Square, Ellon, in 1836. [NRS.AD14.36.170]

ROBERTSON, ALEXANDER, of Hazelhead, MD, born 1733, died in Aberdeen in 1816. [AJ.5.4.1816]

ROBERTSON, ALEXANDER, born 13 May 1772, son of William Robertson and his wife Jean Ross in Aberdeen, was educated at Marischal College, Aberdeen, from 1786 to 1787, emigrated to New York in 1792 as a painter, married Janet McLaren on 6 August 1806, Secretary of the American Academy of Fine Arts, died in New York on 27 May 1841. [AJ.4877] [MCA]

ROBERTSON, ALEXANDER, son of Archibald Robertson in New York, was educated at Marischal College around 1803. [MCA]

ROBERTSON, ALEXANDER, born 1786, an advocate, died in Aberdeen in 1823. [AJ.10.1.1823]

ROBERTSON, ALEXANDER ALLAN, late a merchant in Aberdeen, died in Nice, Italy, on 29 April 1841. [AJ.4870]

ROBERTSON, ANDREW, son of William Robertson in Aberdeen, graduated MA from Marischal College in 1794. [MCA]

ROBERTSON, ANDREW, a skipper in Aberdeen, inventory, 1809, Comm. Aberdeen. [NRS]

ROBERTSON, ARCHIBALD, born 1764, son of William Robertson in Aberdeen, was educated at King's College in 1783, a portrait painter for forty-four years in New York, Secretary of the American Academy of Fine Arts, died there on 6 December 1835. [AJ.4593][KCA]

ROBERTSON, ARCHIBALD, born 1834, from Woodside, Aberdeen, died in New York on 24 August 1856. [AJ.17.9.1856]

ROBERTSON, BARBARA, born 1728, daughter of Provost John Robertson and sister of Andrew Robertson of Foveran, died in Gallowgate, Aberdeen, in 1803. [AJ.26.5.1803]

ROBERTSON, BENJAMIN, master of the <u>Varoon of Aberdeen</u> from Dundee, with passengers, bound for Sydney, New South Wales, Australia, in November 1853, arrived there on 25 April 1854. [AJ.5516/5651]

ROBERTSON, CHARLES, in Aberdeen, brother of Isaac Robertson a mill carpenter on Richmond Estate, St George, Grenada, testament, 1791, Comm. Aberdeen. [NRS]

ROBERTSON, CHARLES, son of Charles Robertson a merchant in Aberdeen, graduated MA from Marischal College in 1849, joined the Indian Civil Service. [MCA]

ROBERTSON, COLIN, son of the late George Robertson, a merchant, a boy in Robert Gordon's Hospital, was apprenticed to John Leslie, a goldsmith in Aberdeen, from 1785 to 1790. [ACA]

ROBERTSON, FRANCIS, son of the late George Robertson, a merchant, a boy in Robert Gordon's Hospital, was apprenticed to Lewis Wilson, a tailor in Aberdeen, from 1786 to 1791. [ACA]

ROBERTSON, GEORGE, son of the late George Robertson, a merchant, a boy in Robert Gordon's Hospital, was apprenticed to William Farquharson, a saddler in Aberdeen, from 1787 to 1792. [ACA]

ROBERTSON, GEORGE, in Boddams, New Machar, testament, 1794, Comm. Aberdeen. [NRS]

ROBERTSON, GEORGE, was admitted as a baker burgess of Old Aberdeen on 28 October 1811. [ACA]

ROBERTSON, JAMES, was admitted as a burgess of Old Aberdeen on 25 October 1819. [ACA]

ROBERTSON, JAMES, born 1753 in Yell, was educated at Aberdeen Grammar School, graduated MA from Marischal College, Aberdeen, in 1778, a land surveyor in Jamaica, mapped Jamaica in 1790s, and north east Scotland in the 1810s. [ACA]

ROBERTSON, JAMES, born 11 March 1769, son of George Robertson and his wife Ann Allan in Aberdeen, was educated at King's College, Aberdeen, from 1786 to 1790, a surgeon in Jamaica. [KCA]

ROBERTSON, JOHN, was admitted as a blacksmith burgess of Old Aberdeen on 25 January 1802. [ACA]

ROBERTSON, JOHN, was admitted as a cooper burgess of Old Aberdeen on 26 October 1812. [ACA]

ROBERTSON, MARY, spouse of Bishop Skinner of Aberdeen, died there in 1807. [AJ.4.3.1807]

ROBERTSON, MARY, born 1735, widow of Dr Thomas Robertson a physician in Aberdeen, died there in 1816. [AJ.10.1.1816]

ROBERTSON, PATRICK, from Old Machar, was educated at King's College in 1841, later a teacher in Aberdeen. [KCA]

ROBERTSON, PETER, was admitted as a staymaker burgess of Old Aberdeen on 6 October 1796. [ACA]

ROBERTSON, PETER, a teacher in Aberdeen, father of John Robertson who was educated at Marischal College in1856, later was a solicitor in Galt, Ontario. [MCA]

ROBERTSON, RACHEL, widow of William White a merchant in Aberdeen, sister and heir of Adam Topp in Jamaica, who died 26 August 1868. [NRS.S/H]

ROBERTSON, SARAH JANE, third daughter of George Robertson in Aberdeen, married James Moir Forbes, editor of the *Aberdeen Journal* in Quebec on 23 October 1838. [AJ.4744]

ROBERTSON, THOMAS, born 1768 in Aberdeen, a Customs Officer and city surveyor, died in Savanna, Georgia on 27 December 1810. [Savanna Daily Recorder]

ROBERTSON, WILLIAM, was admitted as a trade burgess of Old Aberdeen on 31 October 1825. [ACA]

ROBIE, DAVID, was admitted as a weaver burgess of Old Aberdeen on 27 October 1806. [ACA]

ROGER, CATHERINE, in Aberdeen, daughter of John Roger and his wife Janet Donald, testament, 1797, Comm. Aberdeen. [NRS]

ROGER, JOHN MORRICE, from Aberdeen, was educated at King's College, Aberdeen, later a minister in Peterborough, Canada. [KCA]

RONALD, FORBES, born 1797, an apprentice from Aberdeen, was drowned in the wreck of the whaling ship Oscar of Aberdeen in 1813. [AJ]

RONALDS, MARGARET, eldest daughter of John Ronalds in Aberdeen, married William Pallen in Bathurst, New Brunswick, on 11 July 1841. [St Andrews Standard, 30.7.1841]

ROSE, ANNE, relict of George Lobban a landwaiter in Aberdeen, testament, 1795, Comm. Aberdeen. [NRS]

ROSE, DONALDSON, of Hazelhead, born 1780, a merchant in Aberdeen, died at 11 Golden Square, Aberdeen, in 1853. [AJ.1.4.1853]

ROSE Reverend HUGH JAMES, Principal of King's College, Aberdeen, died in Florence, Italy, on 22 December 1838. [AJ]

ROSE, ROBERT GORDON, son of Charles Gordon Rose of Blelack, died in Aberdeen in 1824. [AJ.2.7.1824]

ROSS, ALEXANDER, son of Finlay Ross in Aberdeen, was apprenticed to Peter Duncan, a weaver in Aberdeen, from 1787 to 1792. [ACA]

ROSS, CHARLES, a merchant in Aberdeen, father of George Ross a magistrate in Demerara, 1843. [NRS.S/H]

ROSS, GEORGE, son of Alexander Ross, a carter to Strachan, Imray and Company at New Bridge, Aberdeen, was apprenticed to William Strachan, a baker in Aberdeen, from 1788 to 1795. [ACA]

ROSS, GEORGE, a planter in Jamaica, brother and heir of John Ross an advocate in Aberdeen, 1797. [NRS.S/H]

ROSS, GEORGE, son of John Ross a coachbuilder in Aberdeen, was educated at Marischal College in 1848, later with the Oriental Bank in Hong Kong, afterwards in Sydney, New South Wales, Australia. [MCA]

ROSS, JAMES, was found guilty of attempted rape and assault in Aberdeen in 1815, and was sentenced to transportation to the colonies for life. [NRS.GD1.959]

ROSS, JAMES, the burgh drummer, was admitted as a burgess of Old Aberdeen on 2 October 1817. [ACA]

ROSS, JOHN LEITH, of Arnage and Bourtrie, born 1777, died in Bon Accord Square, Aberdeen, in 1839. [AJ.15.5.1839]

ROSS, MARY, wife of William Allardyce a wine merchant, died at Crown Street, Aberdeen, in 1835, as did their daughter Elizabeth Young Allardyce born 1831. [AJ.3.4.1835]

ROSS, PETER, a mason in Aberdeen, testament, 1800, Comm. Aberdeen. [NRS]

ROSS, ROBERT, was admitted as a merchant burgess of Old Aberdeen on 28 October 1799. [ACA]

ROSS, ROBERT, son of John Ross a merchant in Aberdeen, died in Cape Town, Cape of Good Hope, South Africa, in 1810. [EA.4832]

ROSS, ROBERT, was admitted as a druggist burgess of Old Aberdeen on 27 October 1855. [ACA]

ROSS, WILLIAM, son of Alexander Ross in Aberdeen, died in St George, Grenada, on 10 October 1806. [SM.68.564]

ROUGH, HELEN, in Aberdeen, testament, 1790, Comm. Aberdeen. [NRS]

ROW, ANN, daughter of Thomas Row a merchant in Aberdeen, married George Laing from Winchester, Upper Canada, on 14 November 1836. [AJ.4637]

ROWE, JOHN, was admitted as a mariner burgess of Old Aberdeen on 14 November 1801. [ACA]

ROWELL, JOSEPH, born 1808, from Aberdeen, died in Norra Gurda, Gothenburg, Sweden, on 8 June 1867. [AJ.6231]

ROY, JEAN, in Aberdeen, testament, 1791, Comm. Aberdeen. [NRS]

RUNCY, CHARLES FREDERICK, son of Charles Runcy a merchant in Aberdeen, graduated MA from Marischal College in 1846, an advocate in Aberdeen in 1855. [MCA]

RUNCIE, GEORGE, in Aberdeen, graduated MD from King's College, Aberdeen, on 6 April 1847. [KCA]

RUSSELL, Captain JOHN, of the Royal Navy, eldest son of Thomas Russell of Rathe, died in Aberdeen in 1813. [AJ.13.11.1814]; inventory, 1814, Comm. Aberdeen. [NRS]

RUSSELL, Captain, master of the Heroine of Aberdeen from the River Clyde bound for Chaleur Bay, New Brunswick, in 1840. [GA.5625]

SALMON, JOHN, born 1801, a seaman in Aberdeen, was accused of housebreaking and theft in 1817. [NRS.AC17.14.40],

SAMUEL, GEORGE ROBERT, son of Peter Samuel, a Wesleyan preacher in Aberdeen, was educated at Marischal College in 1848. [MCA]

SAMUEL, PETER, a Wesleyan preacher in Aberdeen, was educated at Marischal College in 1845. [MCA]

SANDERSON, ALFRED, from Old Machar, graduated MD from King's College in 1849. [MCA]

SANDERSON, GEORGE, born 1763, factor to the Duke of Gordon, died in Aberdeen in1835. [AJ.14.4.1835]

SANDILANDS, PATRICK, a merchant in Aberdeen, testament, 1797, Comm. Aberdeen. [NRS]

SANDISON, ROBERT, an Excise officer in Aberdeen, testament, 1790, Comm. Aberdeen. [NRS]

SANG, WILLIAM, son of William Sang a baker in Aberdeen, settled in Tobago before 1828. [St Nicholas gravestone, Aberdeen]; late from Tobago, died at the Grove, Aberdeen, on 8 July 1842. [AJ.4933]

SANGSTER, JAMES, was admitted as a tailor burgess of Old Aberdeen on 29 October 1792. [ACA]

SANGSTER, JAMES, a butcher in Aberdeen, died in 1843. [AJ.12.10.1843]

SANGSTER, JOHN, son of John Sangster a slater and chimney sweep in Aberdeen, a thief imprisoned in Aberdeen Tolbooth, was sentenced on 1 April 1788 to transportation for fourteen years. [AJ.2102]

SANGSTER, JOHN, was admitted as a merchant burgess of Old Aberdeen on 28 October 1811. [ACA]

SANGSTER, ROBERT, formerly a butcher in Aberdeen, died in Maldon, Victoria, Australia, on 5 December 1866. [AJ.6220]

SANGSTER, THOMAS, was admitted as a burgess of Old Aberdeen on 30 March 1801. [ACA]

SANGSTER, THOMAS, was admitted as an advocate burgess of Old Aberdeen on 4 October 1804. [ACA]

SCORGIE, JOHN, born 1812, arrived in Kingston, Jamaica, on 11 May 1841 on board the Rob Roy from Aberdeen. [TNA.CO140/33]

SCOTLAND, JOHN, a skipper in Aberdeen, inventory, 1820, Comm. Aberdeen. [NRS]

SCOTT, ALEXANDER, son of James Scott a shoemaker in Aberdeen, was educated at Marischal College in 1846. [MCA]

SCOTT, ALEXANDER, in Old Machar, father of Thomas Smith born 27 January 1853, was educated at Aberdeen University in 1872, a chaplain in India from 1881 to 1907. [F.7.580]

SCOTT, JAMES, master of the Berbice of Aberdeen from Aberdeen with passengers bound for Quebec from 1854 to 1857. [AJ]

SCOTT, JESSY or JANET, born 1824, wife of William Cox a private soldier of the 1st Royals, in Aberdeen Barracks, was accused of bigamy in 1850. [NRS.AD14.50.153]

SCOTT, PATRICK, born 1817, son of William Scott in Aberdeen, died in Detroit on 13 September 1849. [AJ.5309]

SCOTT, PETER, born 1807, a butcher in Wales Street, Aberdeen, was accused of murder in 1823. [NRS.AD14.23.209]

SCOTT, THOMAS, born 27 January 1853 in Old Machar, son of Alexander Scott, was educated at Aberdeen University around 1872, a chaplain in India from 1881 to 1907. [F.7.580]

SCOTT, WILLIAM, a watchmaker in London, later in Hardgate, Aberdeen, testament, 1798, Comm. Aberdeen. [NRS]

SCOTT, WILLIAM DONALDSON, from Aberdeen, a banker in New York from 1841 to 1858, died in Aberdeen on 22 August 1883. [ANY]

SCOTT, Mrs, widow of Reverend John Scott, and daughter of Professor Gordon of King's College, Aberdeen, died at Gordon's Dale, Virginia, on 15 July 1802. [EA.4042.02]

SCROGGIE, JOHN, a dyer in Aberdeen, died on 7 October 1836, grandfather of William Scroggie, a merchant in Coleraine, Ireland. [NRS.S/H]

SCROGGS, JOHN, a merchant in Aberdeen, testament, 1790, Comm. Aberdeen. [NRS]

SEIVEWRIGHT, JAMES, son of William Seivewright a merchant in Aberdeen, a student at Marischal College from 1848 to 1851, minister of the Scots Kirk in Melbourne, Victoria, Australia, later in Quebec, Canada. [MCA]

SELBIE, JAMES, was admitted as a wright burgess of Old Aberdeen on 30 September 1805. [ACA]

SELBIE, JAMES, was admitted as a merchant burgess of Old Aberdeen on 8 October 1808. [ACA]

SELBY, JAMES, in Aberdeen, graduated MD from King's College, Aberdeen, in 1809. [KCA]

SETON, ISABELLA, daughter of George Seton of Mounie, and wife of Dr Skene Ogilvy minister of Old Machar, died in Old Aberdeen in 1824. [AJ.6.9.1824]

SHAND, ELIZABETH, daughter of Alexander Shand an advocate in Aberdeen, wife of Reverend George Morgan, died in Somerset, Cape of Good Hope, South Africa, on 30 November 1832. [AJ.4440]

SHAND, GEORGE, in Demerara, later in Aberdeen, husband of Mary Walker, testament, 1793, Comm. Aberdeen. [NRS]

SHAND, JAMES, son of Alexander Shand an advocate in Aberdeen, graduated MA from Marischal College in 1816, later a merchant in Java, Dutch East Indies. [MCA]

SHAND, JOHN, son of Alexander Shand a merchant in Aberdeen, died in New York on 6 April 1851. [AJ.14.5.1851]

SHAND, JOSEPH, son of John Shand a miller in Aberdeen, was educated at Marischal College in 1847, later a distiller in Monymusk. [MCA]

SHAND, ROBERT, of Hillside, born 1772, died at 42 Queen Street, Aberdeen, in 1847. [AJ.13.12.1847]

SHAND, Mrs, born 1724, widow of George Shand a former Provost of Aberdeen, died there in 1800. [AJ.29.4.1800]

SHARTY, ANN, in Garden's Close, Castle Street, Aberdeen, was accused of fraudulently using soldiers passes in 1814. [NRS.AD14.14.40]

SHAW, FRANCIS, from Aberdeen, was educated at King's College in 1841, later an antiquary. [KCA]

SHEED, GEORGE, born 28 September 1790, son of George Sheed and his wife Isobel Murray in St Nicholas parish, Aberdeen, was educated at Marischal College, Aberdeen, in 1807, minister of Ancaster and Flamborough, Ontario, from 1827 until his death in 1832. [F.7.650]

SHEIR, JAMES, son of David Sheir a land surveyor in Aberdeen, was educated at Marischal College in 1846. [MCA]

SHEPHERD, FRANCIS, born 1838 in Aberdeen, died in Colesberg, Cape of Good Hope, South Africa, on 26 January 1863. [AJ.6065]

SHEPHERD, JAMES, was admitted as a trade burgess of Old Aberdeen in October 1816. [ACA]

SHEPHERD, MARGARET, widow of David Gill a shoemaker in Aberdeen, testament, 1796, Comm. Aberdeen. [NRS]

SHEPHERD, WILLIAM, born 1736, a former baillie of Aberdeen, died there in 1825. [AJ.2.9.1825]

SHEPPARD, JAMES, born 1830, eldest son of Charles L. Sheppard of 1 Rosemount Place, Aberdeen, died in Wainku, Auckland, New Zealand, on 21 November 1861. [AJ.5955]

SHERRIFF, ALEXANDER, a merchant in Aberdeen, testament, 1793, Comm. Aberdeen. [NRS]

SHERRIFS, DAVID, second son of Convenor David Sheriffs of Aberdeen, an Assemblyman in Jamaica, Lieutenant Colonel of Militia there, died in Kingston, Jamaica, in 1805. [AJ.4.9.1805]

SHERRIFFS, JAMES, a minister in Aberdeen, graduated DD from King's College, Aberdeen, on 23 October 1795. [KCA]

SHERRIFFS, JAMES, was admitted as a trade burgess of Old Aberdeen on 22 December 1823. [ACA]

SHERIFFS, JOHN, in Whiteburn, Nova Scotia, brother and heir of James Sheriffs a court-house keeper in Aberdeen, 1841. [NRS.S/H]

SHIER, JAMES, son of David Shier a land surveyor in Aberdeen, was educated at Marischal College around 1850, later a schoolmaster in New Jersey. [MCA]

SHINIE, GEORGE, was admitted as a merchant burgess of Old Aberdeen on 29 October 1798. [ACA]

SHIRREFS, ALEXANDER, born 1760, died in Aberdeen in 1823. [AJ.22.7.1823]

SHIRREFFS, ALEXANDER, born 1833, late of Aberdeen, died in Bon Accord, Rondebosche, South Africa, on 23 January 1876. [AJ.6684]

SHIRREFS, Reverend Dr, of Friendville, born 1751, died in Aberdeen in 1830. [AJ.26.3.1830]

SHIRREFFS, CHARLES EDWARD, son of Major Alexander Shirreffs in the Service of the Honourable East India Company, was educated at Marischal College in 1854, an Ensign in HEICS, later in New Zealand and Melbourne, Victoria, Australia. [MCA]

SHIRREFFS, DAVID, son of David Shirreffs the Convenor of Aberdeen, settled in St George, Jamaica, died in Kingston, Jamaica on 4 September 1805. [SM.67.967]

SHIRREFFS, JOHN DAVID, a surgeon, eldest son of Alexander Shirreffs an advocate in Aberdeen, died in Port Antonio, Jamaica, on 28 November 1824. [DPCA.1178]

SHORT, JOHN, was admitted as a draff burgess of Old Aberdeen on 8 October 1808. [ACA]

SEIVEWRIGHT, JAMES, son of William Sievewright a merchant in Aberdeen, was educated at Marischal College in 1848, later a minister in Melbourne, Victoria, Australia, and in Quebec. [MCA]

SILVER, BURNETTE, wife of Dr Keith, died at 257 Union Street, Aberdeen, in 1853. [AJ.25.3.1853]

SIM, ALEXANDER, son of Alexander Sim a weaver in Aberdeen, was educated at Marischal College between 1840 and 1843, later a Congregational minister in Canada. [MCA]

SIM, CATHERINE, born 1837, grand-daughter of Reverend D. Sim in Aberdeen, died in Brooklyn, New York, in 1872. [AJ.3.10.1872]

SIM, Reverend DAVID, born 1765, minister of the Union Chapel of Ease in Aberdeen, died in 1823. [AJ.3.1.1823]

SIM, JAMES, master of the <u>Bon Accord of Aberdeen</u> from Aberdeen with passengers bound for Quebec in 1841. [AJ]; master of the <u>Sarah of Aberdeen</u> from Aberdeen with passengers bound for Quebec in 1852. [QM][IJ]

SIM, JAMES, son of James Sim in Aberdeen, was educated at Marischal College in 1855, later a druggist. [MCA]

SIM, JESAMINE, daughter of George Sim in Aberdeen, and wife of Joseph Nelson, died in New York on 23 April 1823. [EA]

SIM, JOHN, son of James Sim, a shipmaster in Aberdeen, settled in Happy Grove, Jamaica, died in Kingston, Jamaica, on 7 April 1811. [DPCA.467][EA.4958]

SIM, JOHN, born 1791, an advocate, died in 1823. [AJ.7.10.1823]

SIM, MARY ANN, born 1800, wife of Charles Phillips a shipmaster, died in Aberdeen in 1832. [AJ.28.8.1832]

SIM, WILLIAM, born 1797, a brewer in Hardgate, Aberdeen, died in 1834. [AJ.29.5.1834]

SIMPSON, ALEXANDER, cashier of the Aberdeen Banking Company, testament, 1794, Comm. Aberdeen. [NRS]

SIMPSON, ALEXANDER, in Gibraltar, later in Aberdeen, an inventory, 3 August 1807, Aberdeen. [NRS.CC1.W321]

SIMPSON, ALEXANDER, born in Aberdeen, emigrated to New Brunswick in 1819, settled in St John, died 1829. [NBC.5.9.1829]

SIMPSON, ALEXANDER, son of Reverend Alexander Simpson in New Machar, was educated at King's College, Aberdeen, from 1812 to 1820, settled in Jamaica. [KCA]

SIMPSON, ALEXANDER, born 1783, late of Simpson and Whyte, died at 15 Bon Accord Square, Aberdeen, in 1852. [AJ.7.11.1852]

SIMPSON, ALEXANDER, son of Alexander Simpson a merchant in Aberdeen, graduated MA from Marischal College in 1843, and MD in 1852. [MCA]

SIMPSON, ALEXANDER, son of William Simpson of Glen Ythan an advocate in Aberdeen, was educated at Marischal College in 1841, an advocate in Aberdeen in 1848. [MCA]

SIMPSON, ANDREW, born 1751, a merchant in Aberdeen, died in 1809. [AJ.6.9.1809]

SIMPSON, ANDREW, was admitted as a wright burgess of Old Aberdeen on 3 October 1839. [ACA]

SIMPSON, CHARLES STEWART STILL, son of William Simpson an advocate, was educated at Marischal College in 1851. [MCA]

SIMPSON, DAVID KINNAIRD, son of William Simpson a shoe maker in Aberdeen, was educated at Marischal College in 1858. [MCA]

SIMPSON, ELSPET, wife of Donaldson Rose a merchant in Aberdeen, died at Knockhall in 1828. [AJ.5.9.1828]

SIMPSON, GEORGE, son of William Simpson a fiscal in Aberdeen, was educated at Marischal College in 1857, settled in New Zealand. [MCA]

SIMPSON, Dr JAMES, 'in the prime of life', died in Aberdeen on 9 May 1820. [SM.86.95]

SIMPSON, JAMES, [1821-1895], in Aberdeen, father of William Simpson, born 1864, died in Guttenberg, New Jersey, on 15 October 1904. [St Clement's gravestone, Aberdeen]

SIMPSON, JAMES, son of William Simpson a fiscal in Aberdeen, was educated at Marischal College in 1857, later a Major of the Royal Engineers. [MCA]

SIMPSON, JANET, wife of Reverend Alexander Spence, died at Castlehill, Aberdeen, in 1850. [AJ.14.8.1850]

SIMPSON, JOHN, was admitted as a merchant burgess of Old Aberdeen on 29 October 1798. [ACA]

SIMPSON, JOHN, a skipper in Aberdeen, inventory, 1822, Comm. Aberdeen. [NRS]

SIMPSON, JOHN, son of John Simpson a merchant in Aberdeen, was educated at Marischal College in 1842, graduated MD from King's College in 1848. [MCA][KCA]

SIMPSON, JOHN, was admitted as a merchant burgess of Old Aberdeen on 25 October 1851. [ACA]

SIMPSON, JOHN, son of Alexander Simpson, a merchant in Aberdeen, was educated at Marischal College in 1850s, later a Presbyterian minister in Australia. [MCA]

SIMPSON, JOSEPH, in Grenada, nephew and heir of Christian Bennet, widow of William Durward a merchant in Aberdeen, in 1800. [NRS.S/H]

SIMPSON, PATRICK STILL, son of William Simpson of Glen Ythan an advocate in Aberdeen, was educated at Marischal College in 1841. [MCA]

SIMPSON, PETER, a merchant in Aberdeen, testament, 1800, Comm. Aberdeen. [NRS]

SIMPSON, SIMON, son of William Simpson an advocate in Aberdeen, was educated at Marischal College in 1854, later a Colonel of the Royal Artillery. [MCA]

SIMPSON, WILLIAM, a druggist, formerly a precentor and teacher of sacred music in Aberdeen, died in St John, Newfoundland, on 12 January 1844. [AJ.5063]

SINGER, ADAM, a merchant in Aberdeen, testament, 1799, Comm. Aberdeen. [NRS]

SIMPSON, Captain, master of the George Canning of Aberdeen landed in Otago, New Zealand, on 29 November 1857. [AJ.5749]

SINCLAIR, GEORGE, son of William Sinclair a druggist in Aberdeen, was educated at Marischal College in 1857. [MCA]

SINCLAIR, WILLIAM, son of William Sinclair a druggist in Aberdeen, graduated MA from Marischal College in 1846, later a wholesale druggist in Aberdeen. [MCA]

SIVEWRIGHT, JAMES, MA, born 1823, from Aberdeen, died in Auckland, New Zealand, on 16 April 1876. [AJ.6705]

SKAKEL, ALEXANDER, from Aberdeen, graduated MA from King's College, Aberdeen, in 1794, a master of the Royal Grammar School of Montreal, Quebec. [KCA]

SKENE, ALEXANDER, of Carraldston, born 1766, died in Aberdeen in 1827. [AJ.30.4.1827]

SKENE, ALEXANDER, son of Charles Skene the Professor of Medicine at Marischal College, was educated there around 1830, later a Captain in the Service of the East India Company, who, with his wife and children, was killed during the Indian Mutiny in 1857. [MCA]

SKENE, ANDREW, fourth son of Captain James Skene in Aberdeen, a Lieutenant of the 60th Regiment, died in Jamaica in 1808. [EA.4702]

SKENE, CHARLES, son of Professor Charles Skene, graduated MA from Marischal College in 1830, later a Captain of the 79th Highlanders and Superintendent of Indians in Canada, [MCA]

SKENE, CHARLES, son of Captain William Skene in Aberdeen, was educated at Marischal College in 1857. [MCA]

SKENE, Dr CHARLES, died at 214 Union Street West, Aberdeen, in 1844. [AJ.11.5.1844]

SKENE, Dr GEORGE, born 1741, a physician in Aberdeen, died in 1803. [AJ.25.3.1803]

SKENE, JAMES, in Aberdeen, former Captain of the 98th Regiment of Foot, testament, 1797, Comm. Aberdeen. [NRS]

SKENE, JOHN DUNCAN, from Aberdeen, son of Thomas Skene the Inspector of the Poor in Old Machar, was educated at Marischal College in 1852, later a commercial agent in San Francisco, California. [MCA]

SKENE, Lieutenant Colonel JOHN GORDON CUMMING, died in Aberdeen in 1828. [AJ.6.4.1828]

SKINNER, JEAN, born 1765, eldest daughter of Bishop Skinner of Aberdeen, died in Aberdeen in 1824. [AJ.22.6.1824]

SKINNER, Reverend JOHN, born 1731, Episcopalian minister of Longside, died at the home of his son Bishop John Skinner in Aberdeen in 1807. [AJ.16.6.1807]

SKINNER, JOHN, born 1743, Senior Bishop and Primus if the Scottish Episcopal Church, died in Aberdeen in 1816. [AJ.13.7.1816]

SKUES, EDWARD WALKER, son of George Skues a Lieutenant of the Royal Marines in Aberdeen, was educated at Marischal College in 1844. [MCA]

SKUES, FREDERICK MACKENZIE, from Aberdeen, son of George Skues a Lieutenant of the Royal Marines, was educated at Marischal College in 1840S, later of Snell Hall Estate, Calcutta, India. [MCA]

SKUES, WILLIAM MACKENZIE, from Aberdeen, son of George Skues a Lieutenant of the Royal Marines, was educated at Marischal College in 1851. [MCA]

SMART, Captain, master of the Heroine of Aberdeen from Dundee with passengers bound for New York in 1831, 1832. [DPCA]; master of the Moira of Aberdeen from Leith to Melbourne, Victoria, Australia, on 18 August 1859, landed there on 27 December 1859. [AJ.825]

SMITH, ADAM, an advocate in Demerara, died 14 September 1812, brother of Margaret Smith in Aberdeen, testament, 1814, Comm. Edinburgh. [NRS]

SMITH, ALEXANDER, son of William Smith a slater in Aberdeen, was apprenticed to John Leslie a goldsmith in Aberdeen from 1789 to 1796. [ACA]

SMITH, ALEXANDER, son of Alexander Smith, a carter on Schoolhill, Aberdeen, was apprenticed to William Bain, a weaver in Aberdeen, from 1794 to 1799. [ACA]

SMITH, ALEXANDER, jr., was admitted as a merchant burgess of Old Aberdeen on 29 October 1798. [ACA]

SMITH, ALEXANDER, only son of Alexander Smith a papermaker in Stoneywood, died in Aberdeen in 1800. [AJ.11.1.1800]

SMITH, ALEXANDER, was admitted as a blacksmith burgess of Old Aberdeen on 25 October 1813. [ACA]

SMITH, ALEXANDER, jr., was admitted as a merchant burgess of Old Aberdeen on 29 October 1798. [ACA]

SMITH, ALEXANDER, was admitted as a trade burgess of Old Aberdeen on 30 October 1820. [ACA]

SMITH, ALEXANDER, was admitted as a merchant burgess of Old Aberdeen on 31 October 1825. [ACA]

SMITH, ALEXANDER, was admitted as a merchant burgess of Old Aberdeen on 3 October 1832. [ACA]

SMITH, ALEXANDER, was admitted as a salmon fisher burgess of Old Aberdeen on 13 December 1837. [ACA]

SMITH, ALEXANDER, son of David Smith in Aberdeen, graduated MA from Marischal College in 1846. [MCA]

SMITH, Captain ALEXANDER, from Aberdeen, master of the Charlotte of Belfast, died in New Orleans on 10 March 1848. [AJ.5233]

SMITH, ALEXANDER, an engineer from Aberdeen, married Jane Cameron, daughter of David Cameron an iron funder in Bahia, Brazil, at HM Consulate there on 5 December 1863. [AJ.6053]

SMITH, ALEXANDER PHILIP, son of Lewis Smith a bookseller in Aberdeen, was educated at Marischal College in 1856, later with the General Accident Assurance Company in Perth. [MCA]

SMITH, ANDREW, a draper in Aberdeen, father of John Gould Smith, educated at Marischal College in 1854, a minister in Pietermaritzberg, Natal, South Africa, from 1877 until 1903, died on 31 February 1913. [MCA] [F.7.564]

SMITH, ANN, wife of Alexander Beaton, from Aberdeen, died in Rotterdam in the Netherlands on 19 February 1841. [AJ.4861]

SMITH, ARCHIBALD, born 1810, with Christian Smith, born 1811, Craick Smith, born 1833, and John Smith, born 1835, arrived in Kingston, Jamaica, on 11 May 1841 on board the Rob Roy from Aberdeen. [TNA.CO140/33]

SMITH, CHRISTIANA, daughter of John Smith in Aberdeen, married James Ross, in Halifax, Nova Scotia, on 5 June 1825. [AR.11.6.1825]

SMITH, COLVIN, from Aberdeen, graduated MD from King's College, Aberdeen, on 11 April 1851. [KCA]

SMITH, DANIEL, born 1799 in Aberdeen, died in Longueli, Ottawa, on 17 April 1848. [AJ.5237]

SMITH, GEORGE, was admitted as a merchant burgess of Old Aberdeen on 8 October 1808. [ACA]

SMITH, GEORGE, was admitted as a blacksmith burgess of Old Aberdeen on 30 October 1809. [ACA]

SMITH, GEORGE, born 1811 in Aberdeen, an assistant in the Bhowanipore Factory, Bengal, India, died 22 May 1842. [Blowanipure gravestone]

SMITH, GEORGE, was admitted as a mason burgess of Old Aberdeen on 26 October 1829. [ACA]

SMITH, GEORGE E., son of Jeremiah Smith, was admitted as a burgess of Old Aberdeen on 23 March 1837. [ACA]

SMITH, GEORGE, third son of George Smith in Aberdeen, a surgeon of the 33rd Native Infantry Regiment, died in Guntoor, India, on 19 November 1838. [AJ.4752]

SMITH, GAVIN MITCHELL, born 1813, died in Aberdeen in 1842. [AJ.4.1.1843]

SMITH, HUGH, born 1821, youngest son of Mr Smith in Nether Kirkgait, Aberdeen, died in Sydney, New South Wales, Australia, on 19 September 1855. [AJ.5635]

SMITH, ISABEL, wife of John Smith, Gallowgate, parish of St Nicholas, Aberdeen, a victim of crime in 1825. [NRS.JC26.1825.29]

SMITH, ISABELLA, daughter of George Smith in Aberdeen, married Reverend George Milne MA, a missionary of the Society for the Propagation of the Gospel, in Quebec Cathedral on 17 October 1842. [AJ.4950]

SMITH, JAMES, born 1767, Superintendent of the Aberdeenshire Canal, died in Aberdeen in 1841. [AJ.21.2.1841]

SMITH, JAMES, was admitted as a merchant burgess of Old Aberdeen on 26 October 1812. [ACA]

SMITH, JAMES, was admitted as a trade burgess of Old Aberdeen on 27 November 1824. [ACA]

SMITH, JAMES, from Aberdeen, graduated MA from King's College, Aberdeen, on 31 March 1826, later a schoolmaster in Keith. [KCA]

SMITH, JAMES, from Aberdeen, graduated MA from King's College, Aberdeen, on 31 March 1826, later a minister in Ellon. [KCA]

SMITH, JAMES, son of Alexander Smith a merchant in Aberdeen, graduated MA from Marischal College in 1840. [MCA]

SMITH, JAMES, son of Alexander Smith, born 1779, died 19 March 1827, a shoemaker in Aberdeen and his wife Isabella Main, settled in Buffalo, New York. [Banchory Ternan gravestone]

SMITH, JAMES, born 1775, formerly a seedsman in Aberdeen, died in Naryton, Brantford, Canada West, on 12 June 1844. [AJ.5036]

SMITH, JAMES, was admitted as a burgess of Old Aberdeen on 24 April 1852. [ACA]

SMITH, JAMES LAMOND, from Glen Millan, Aberdeen, married Isabella Barker, third daughter of George Barker of Leamington Priory, Warwickshire, in Guelph, Canada, on 22 October 1844. [SM.ns.23.196]

SMITH, JEREMIAH, was admitted as a blacksmith burgess of Old Aberdeen on 24 April 1827. [ACA]

SMITH, JOHN, late in Antigua, died in Aberdeen, testament, 1795, Comm. Aberdeen. [NRS]

SMITH, JOHN, a pewterer and auctioneer in Aberdeen, testament, 1799, Comm. Aberdeen. [NRS]

SMITH, JOHN, a merchant in Aberdeen, testament, 1800, Comm. Aberdeen. [NRS]

SMITH, JOHN, was admitted as a blacksmith burgess of Old Aberdeen on 25 January 1802. [ACA]

SMITH, JOHN, in Woodside, was admitted as a merchant burgess of Old Aberdeen on 10 November 1803. [ACA]

SMITH, JOHN, was admitted as a trade burgess of Old Aberdeen in October 1816. [ACA]

SMITH, JOHN, a skipper in Aberdeen, inventory, 1821, Comm. Aberdeen. [NRS]

SMITH, JOHN, was admitted as a merchant burgess of Old Aberdeen on 31 October 1825. [ACA]

SMITH, JOHN, was admitted as a shoemaker burgess of Old Aberdeen on 7 May 1829. [ACA]

SMITH, JOHN ROBERT, of Concraig, born 1807, died in Aberdeen in 1824. [AJ.25.12.1824]

SMITH, JOHN, master of the <u>Malvina of Aberdeen</u> from Aberdeen with passengers bound for Canada, in 1811. [NRS.E504.1.24]

SMITH, JOHN, stabler and vintner, Gallowgate, parish of St Nicholas, Aberdeen, a victim of crime in 1825. [NRS.JC26.1825.29]

SMITH, JOHN, son of John Smith a tailor in Aberdeen, settled in Melbourne, Victoria, Australia, by 1853. [NRS.S/H]

SMITH, JOHN, from Aberdeen, son of Andrew Smith, a draper, was educated at Marischal College in 1854, graduated MA, a minister in Pietermaritzburg, South Africa. [MCA]

SMITH, JOHN, a wood carver in Aberdeen, father of Annie Smith who married Dr T. Fenwick in Nelson, New Zealand, on 4 January 1872. [AJ.6481]

SMITH, JOSEPH, born 1804, son of Reverend Joseph Smith in Birse, died in Aberdeen in 1823. [AJ.21.2.1823]

SMITH, KATHERINE, in Aberdeen, relict of John Mitchell sometime in Foveran, Aberdeenshire, testament, 1794, Comm. Aberdeen. [NRS]

SMITH, MARGARET, born 1817, daughter of John Smith, a writer in Huntly, and wife of Alexander Gordon, died in Madoc, Upper Canada, on 21 October 1848. [AJ.5264]

SMITH, MARY, daughter of John Smith, Gallowgate, parish of St Nicholas, Aberdeen a victim of crime in 1825. [NRS.JC26.1825.29]

SMITH, MARY LOUISA, daughter of Alexander Smith a merchant in Aberdeen, married Peter Smith from Albany, New York, there on 15 February 1860. [AJ.5851]; heir to her father who died 15 June 1870. [NRS.S/H]

SMITH, PETER, born 1792, a coppersmith from Aberdeen, died in 16 Beaver Street, Albany, New York, on 16 February 1858. [AJ.17.3.1858]

SMITH, ROBERT, a skipper in Aberdeen, inventory, 1822, Comm. Aberdeen. [NRS]

SMITH, ROBERT PRIMROSE, son of David Smith a seaman in Aberdeen, was educated at Marischal College in 1855, later was a minister in Canada and New Zealand. [MCA]

SMITH, RODERICK, was admitted as a blacksmith burgess of Old Aberdeen on 2 November 1807. [ACA]

SMITH, SAMUEL, son of John Smith a tailor in Aberdeen, was educated at Marischal College in 1852, later was a surgeon in Kyneton, Victoria, Australia. [MCA]

SMITH, THOMAS, was admitted as a merchant burgess of Old Aberdeen on 28 October 1811. [ACA]

SMITH, THOMAS, was admitted as a glazier burgess of Old Aberdeen on 29 October 1832. [ACA]

SMITH, WILLIAM, born 1754 in Aberdeen, son of William Smith, emigrated to America as an Episcopalian clergyman, died in New York on 6 April 1821. [WA]

SMITH, WILLIAM, was admitted as a salmon fisher burgess of Old Aberdeen on 29 October 1792. [ACA]

SMITH, WILLIAM, son of William Smith, a slater in Aberdeen, was apprenticed to Peter Robertson, a staymaker in Aberdeen, from 1785 to 1792. [ACA]

SMITH, WILLIAM, jr., a merchant in Aberdeen, testament, 1796, Comm. Aberdeen. [NRS]

SMITH, WILLIAM, from Aberdeen, was educated at King's College, Aberdeen, from 1798 to 1802, a teacher in New York from 1806 to 1816, died in Port Jackson, Australia, in 1826. [ANY]

SMITH, WILLIAM, was admitted as a trade burgess of Old Aberdeen on 17 March 1806. [ACA]

SMITH, WILLIAM, was admitted as a merchant burgess of Old Aberdeen on 8 October 1808. [ACA]

SMITH, WILLIAM, was admitted as a merchant burgess of Old Aberdeen on 18 January 1819. [ACA]

SMITH, WILLIAM, was admitted as a blacksmith burgess of Old Aberdeen on 13 December 1837. [ACA]

SMITH, WILLIAM, a surgeon, died in Footdee, Aberdeen, in 1841. [AJ.8.4.1841]

SMITH, WILLIAM, from Aberdeen, son of David Smith a shipmaster, was educated at Marischal College in 1852. [MCA]

SMITH, YEOMAN, son of William Smith in Clayhills, Aberdeen, a butcher who died in Sydney, New South Wales, Australia, on 25 June 1872. [AJ.9507]

SMITH, ..., and his wife Agnes Moir, both from Aberdeen, residing at 294 Washington Street, New York, on 9 April 1837. [AJ.4676]

SMYTH, LESLIE, born in Aberdeen, was naturalised in Newberry County, South Carolina, on 22 April 1843. [SCA]; married Ann Matilda O'Hanlon, daughter of Terence O'Hanlon, in Columbia, South Carolina, by Reverend Malcolm McPherson on 6 February 1838. [AJ.4707]

SNAWIE, ELSPETH, a prisoner in Aberdeen Tolbooth, was banished from Scotland on 20 September 1800. [NRS.JC11.44]

SOUTAR, ALEXANDER, was admitted as a blacksmith burgess of Old Aberdeen on 29 October 1821. [ACA]

SPALDING, JAMES, born 1777, son of Robert Spalding a hairdresser in Aberdeen, a writer in Aberdeen, was admitted as a Notary Public on 29 June 1796, an advocate, died in Aberdeen on 3 June 1812. [AJ.3.6.1812][NRS.NP2.35.343]

SPARK, THOMAS, born 1756, Treasurer of Aberdeen Infirmary, died 1848. [AJ.19.3.1848]

STABLES, ADAM, was admitted as a merchant burgess of Old Aberdeen, on 31 October 1803, [ACA]; Convenor of the Incorporated Trades of Old Aberdeen, died in 1833. [AJ.17.4.1833]

STABLES, ADAM, eldest son of Alexander Stables, was admitted as a merchant burgess of Old Aberdeen on 14 November 1835. [ACA]

STABLES, ALEXANDER, was admitted as a merchant burgess of Old Aberdeen on 30 October 1820. [ACA]

STABLES, ALEXANDER, jr., was admitted as a burgess of Old Aberdeen on 25 October 1839. [ACA]

STABLES, GEORGE, was admitted as a merchant burgess of Old Aberdeen on 27 August 1823. [ACA]

STABLES, GEORGE, was admitted as a mason burgess of Old Aberdeen on 31 October 1836. [ACA]

STABLES, GEORGE, was admitted as a burgess of Old Aberdeen on 25 October 1845. [ACA]

STABLES, JAMES, was admitted as a vintner burgess of Old Aberdeen on 29 October 1810. [ACA]

STABLES, JAMES, was admitted as a merchant burgess of Old Aberdeen on 25 October 1851. [ACA]

STABLES, WILLIAM, was admitted as a burgess of Old Aberdeen on 8 October 1808. [ACA]

STARK, JAMES, a nephew of James Ferguson a manufacturer in Aberdeen, and for many years his agent in Halifax, Nova Scotia, died in Oregon Territory in June 1843. [AJ.5012]

STEPHEN, ANNE, born 1748, wife of James Calder a wine merchant, died in Aberdeen in 1829. [AJ.8.12.1829]

STEPHEN, GEORGE, was admitted as a merchant burgess of Old Aberdeen on 30 October 1820. [ACA]

STEVEN, PATRICK, was admitted as a trade burgess of Old Aberdeen in October 1816. [ACA]

STEPHEN, ROBERT, was admitted as a merchant burgess of Old Aberdeen on 10 November 1792. [ACA]

STEPHEN, ROBERT, was admitted as a blacksmith burgess of Old Aberdeen on 24 April 1827. [ACA]

STEPHEN, WILLIAM, was admitted as a weaver burgess of Old Aberdeen on 26 October 1807. [ACA]

STEPHEN, WILLIAM, was admitted as a merchant burgess of Old Aberdeen on 14 November 1817. [ACA]

STEPHEN, WILLIAM, was admitted as a trade burgess of Old Aberdeen on 22 December 1823. [ACA]

STEPHEN, WILLIAM, from Aberdeen, was educated at King's College in 1857, graduated MD. [KCA]

STEPHEN, Captain, master of the Quebec Packet of Aberdeen from Aberdeen with passengers bound for Quebec in 1835. [AJ]

STEVEN, ALEXANDER, son of Alexander Steven in Tobago, a student at Marischal College, Aberdeen, in the 1790s. [MCA]

STEVEN, GEORGE, in Cairnery, Old Machar, testament, 1798, Comm. Aberdeen. [NRS]

STEVENSON, ALEXANDER, skipper of the brigantine Flora of Aberdeen, inventory, 1817, Comm. Aberdeen. [NRS]

STEVENSON, JAMES, was admitted as a shoemaker burgess of Old Aberdeen on 3 February 1859. [ACA]

STEWART, ALEXANDER, son of George Stewart a merchant in Aberdeen, was educated at Marischal College in 1850. [MCA]

STEWART, ARCHIBALD F., minister of Greyfriars, Aberdeen, was educated at Marischal College in 1843. [MCA]

STEWART, ARTHUR, MD, born 1784, Inspector General of Army Hospitals, died at 5 Springbank Terrace, Aberdeen, in 1854. [AJ.28.12.1854]

STEWART, DAVID, from Old Machar, was educated at King's College, Aberdeen, in 1855, became Lord Provost of Aberdeen. [KCA]

STEWART, GEORGE, born 1821, a labourer, with Ann Stewart, born 1823, arrived in Kingston, Jamaica, on 11 May 1841 on board the Rob Roy from Aberdeen. [TNA.CO140/33]

STEWART, HENRY, from Aberdeen, a sailor on the Jupiter of New York, died in California in 1823. [AJ.4036]

SMITH, WILLIAM, a surgeon, died in Footdee, Aberdeen, in 1841. [AJ.8.4.1841]

SMITH, WILLIAM, from Aberdeen, son of David Smith a shipmaster, was educated at Marischal College in 1852. [MCA]

SMITH, YEOMAN, son of William Smith in Clayhills, Aberdeen, a butcher who died in Sydney, New South Wales, Australia, on 25 June 1872. [AJ.9507]

SMITH, ..., and his wife Agnes Moir, both from Aberdeen, residing at 294 Washington Street, New York, on 9 April 1837. [AJ.4676]

SMYTH, LESLIE, born in Aberdeen, was naturalised in Newberry County, South Carolina, on 22 April 1843. [SCA]; married Ann Matilda O'Hanlon, daughter of Terence O'Hanlon, in Columbia, South Carolina, by Reverend Malcolm McPherson on 6 February 1838. [AJ.4707]

SNAWIE, ELSPETH, a prisoner in Aberdeen Tolbooth, was banished from Scotland on 20 September 1800. [NRS.JC11.44]

SOUTAR, ALEXANDER, was admitted as a blacksmith burgess of Old Aberdeen on 29 October 1821. [ACA]

SPALDING, JAMES, born 1777, son of Robert Spalding a hairdresser in Aberdeen, a writer in Aberdeen, was admitted as a Notary Public on 29 June 1796, an advocate, died in Aberdeen on 3 June 1812. [AJ.3.6.1812][NRS.NP2.35.343]

SPARK, THOMAS, born 1756, Treasurer of Aberdeen Infirmary, died 1848. [AJ.19.3.1848]

STABLES, ADAM, was admitted as a merchant burgess of Old Aberdeen, on 31 October 1803, [ACA]; Convenor of the Incorporated Trades of Old Aberdeen, died in 1833. [AJ.17.4.1833]

STABLES, ADAM, eldest son of Alexander Stables, was admitted as a merchant burgess of Old Aberdeen on 14 November 1835. [ACA]

STABLES, ALEXANDER, was admitted as a merchant burgess of Old Aberdeen on 30 October 1820. [ACA]

STABLES, ALEXANDER, jr., was admitted as a burgess of Old Aberdeen on 25 October 1839. [ACA]

STABLES, GEORGE, was admitted as a merchant burgess of Old Aberdeen on 27 August 1823. [ACA]

STABLES, GEORGE, was admitted as a mason burgess of Old Aberdeen on 31 October 1836. [ACA]

STABLES, GEORGE, was admitted as a burgess of Old Aberdeen on 25 October 1845. [ACA]

STABLES, JAMES, was admitted as a vintner burgess of Old Aberdeen on 29 October 1810. [ACA]

STABLES, JAMES, was admitted as a merchant burgess of Old Aberdeen on 25 October 1851. [ACA]

STABLES, WILLIAM, was admitted as a burgess of Old Aberdeen on 8 October 1808. [ACA]

STARK, JAMES, a nephew of James Ferguson a manufacturer in Aberdeen, and for many years his agent in Halifax, Nova Scotia, died in Oregon Territory in June 1843. [AJ.5012]

STEPHEN, ANNE, born 1748, wife of James Calder a wine merchant, died in Aberdeen in 1829. [AJ.8.12.1829]

STEPHEN, GEORGE, was admitted as a merchant burgess of Old Aberdeen on 30 October 1820. [ACA]

STEPHEN, ROBERT, was admitted as a merchant burgess of Old Aberdeen on 10 November 1792. [ACA]

STEPHEN, ROBERT, was admitted as a blacksmith burgess of Old Aberdeen on 24 April 1827. [ACA]

STEPHEN, WILLIAM, was admitted as a weaver burgess of Old Aberdeen on 26 October 1807. [ACA]

STEPHEN, WILLIAM, was admitted as a merchant burgess of Old Aberdeen on 14 November 1817. [ACA]

STEPHEN, WILLIAM, was admitted as a trade burgess of Old Aberdeen on 22 December 1823. [ACA]

STEPHEN, WILLIAM, from Aberdeen, was educated at King's College in 1857, graduated MD. [KCA]

STEPHEN, Captain, master of the Quebec Packet of Aberdeen from Aberdeen with passengers bound for Quebec in 1835. [AJ]

STEVEN, ALEXANDER, son of Alexander Steven in Tobago, a student at Marischal College, Aberdeen, in the 1790s. [MCA]

STEVEN, GEORGE, in Cairnery, Old Machar, testament, 1798, Comm. Aberdeen. [NRS]

STEVEN, PATRICK, was admitted as a trade burgess of Old Aberdeen in October 1816. [ACA]

STEVENSON, ALEXANDER, skipper of the brigantine Flora of Aberdeen, inventory, 1817, Comm. Aberdeen. [NRS]

STEVENSON, JAMES, was admitted as a shoemaker burgess of Old Aberdeen on 3 February 1859. [ACA]

STEWART, ALEXANDER, son of George Stewart a merchant in Aberdeen, was educated at Marischal College in 1850. [MCA]

STEWART, ARCHIBALD F., minister of Greyfriars, Aberdeen, was educated at Marischal College in 1843. [MCA]

STEWART, ARTHUR, MD, born 1784, Inspector General of Army Hospitals, died at 5 Springbank Terrace, Aberdeen, in 1854. [AJ.28.12.1854]

STEWART, DAVID, from Old Machar, was educated at King's College, Aberdeen, in 1855, became Lord Provost of Aberdeen. [KCA]

STEWART, GEORGE, born 1821, a labourer, with Ann Stewart, born 1823, arrived in Kingston, Jamaica, on 11 May 1841 on board the Rob Roy from Aberdeen. [TNA.CO140/33]

STEWART, HENRY, from Aberdeen, a sailor on the Jupiter of New York, died in California in 1823. [AJ.4036]

STUART, JOHN, son of David Stuart in Aberdeen, graduated MA from Marischal College in 1844. [MCA]

STUART, JOHN RENNIE, third son of Charles Stuart a shipmaster in Aberdeen, died in Sydney, New South Wales, Australia, on 11 June 1876. [AJ.6709]

STUART, ROBERT, born 1840, son of A. Stuart of the Broadford Works, Aberdeen, died in Savannah, Georgia, on 24 June 1865. [AJ.23.8.1865]

STUART, WALTER LAWSON, from Aberdeen, son of Alexander Laithers an advocate, was educated in 1852 at Marischal College, later in Foochoo, China. [MCA]

SUTHER, JAMES B. FRASER, born 1841, second son of the Bishop of Aberdeen, died in Pates, New Zealand, on 10 March 1870. [AJ.6386]

SUTHERLAND, ALEXANDER, born 1764, 'a manufacturer in the Green, [Aberdeen], for upwards of 50 years', died in 1843. [AJ.25.12.1843]

SUTHERLAND, ALEXANDER, formerly a druggist in Aberdeen, later of Miller and Company druggists in New York, died on 12 July 1846. [AJ.5143]

SUTHERLAND, ALEXANDER, an Inspector of the Union Bank of Australia, [formerly of the Commercial Bank in Aberdeen], married Isabella Esson, daughter of Francis Ormond, in Geelong, Australia, on 12 January 1871. [AJ.6431]

SUTHERLAND, or CROMBIE, BATHIA, was accused of a bigamous marriage in 1817. [NRS.AD14.17.156]

SUTHERLAND, JOHN, born 1766, a hosier, died in 1847. [AJ.11.12.1847]

SUTHERLAND, THOMAS, son of Robert Sutherland a baker in Aberdeen, was educated at Marischal College in 1848, later Chairman of the P. and O. Steam Navigation Company. [MCA]

SUTHERLAND, WILLIAM, son of Adam Sutherland, was apprenticed to Peter Anderson, a tailor in Aberdeen, from 1794 to 1790. [ACA]

SUTHERLAND, WILLIAM, in Aberdeen, son of Kenneth Sutherland a merchant in Thurso, Caithness, testament, 1798, Comm. Aberdeen. [NRS]

SUTHERLAND, WILLIAM, son of Hugh Sutherland a painter in Aberdeen, graduated MA from Marischal College in 1857 also MB in 1863, settled in Cape Colony, South Africa. [MCA]

SUTHERLAND, Mrs, from Aberdeen, died on board the Isabella on passage from Glasgow to New York on 1 September 1852. [AJ.13.10.1852]

SWANSON, MAGNUS, was admitted as a trade burgess of Old Aberdeen on 30 October 1820. [ACA]

SWAP, JAMES, was admitted as a burgess of Old Aberdeen on 8 October 1808. [ACA]

SYMMERS, ANDREW, son of William Symmers, a porter in Aberdeen, was apprenticed to David Middleton, a weaver in Aberdeen, from 1785 to 1790. [ACA]

SYMMER, GEORGE, late Captain of the 25th Regiment of Foot and barrack-master in Aberdeen, testament, 1796, Comm. Aberdeen. [NRS]

SYMMERS, GEORGE, of Cults, born 1765, died in Aberdeen in 1839. [AJ.22.12.1839]

TAIT, GEORGE BERRY, born 1844, a carpenter on the <u>Ann Duthie of Aberdeen</u>, died in Sydney, New South Wales, Australia, on 19 March 1876. [AJ.6700]

TAIT, MARY, daughter of Charles Tait, advocate, and widow of W. Smith of the Royal Navy, died in Aberdeen in 1838. [AJ.1.4.1838]

TAWSE, ALEXANDER, from Aberdeen, graduated MA from King's College, Aberdeen, on 28 March 1812, later was a surgeon in the Service of the East India Company. [KCA]

TAWS, CHARLES, a cabinetmaker in Aberdeen, emigrated via London to America in 1780s. [SG]

TAYLOR, ALEXANDER, at Haddo House, later in Aberdeen, testament, 1791, Comm. Aberdeen. [NRS]

TAYLOR, ALEXANDER, born 1846, from Aberdeen, died in Oamaru, Otago, New Zealand, on 22 May 1876. [AJ.6707]

TAYLOR, CHRISTIAN, born 1815, wife of John T. Blore MA late of Marischal College, Aberdeen, died at the Cape of Good Hope, South Africa, on 18 February 1839. [AJ.4768]

TAYLOR, ELIZA, born 1827, widow of William Wisely MD, and wife of William Matthews of Pulmuir, died at 261 George Street, Aberdeen, in 1853. [AJ.16.6.1853]

TAYLOR, GEORGE, born 1789, a manufacturer, died at 112 Crown Street, Aberdeen, in 1846. [AJ.13.6.1846]

TAYLOR, JOANNA, born 1828 in Aberdeen, wife of John Ingram, died in Baltimore, Maryland, on 20 January 1860. [AJ.5851]

TAYLOR, JAMES, son of John Taylor a worker in Aberdeen, was educated at Marischal College in 1847, later a surgeon at Pitmuxton. [MCA]

TAYLOR, PETER, was admitted as a farmer burgess of Old Aberdeen on 10 April 1813. [ACA]

TAYLOR, WILLIAM, was admitted as a merchant burgess of Old Aberdeen on 14 November 1799. [ACA]

TEMPLE, ELSPET, in Aberdeen, testament, 1791, Comm. Aberdeen. [NRS]

TEMPLETON, Reverend JAMES, born 1770, of the United Associate Congregation in Belmont Street, Aberdeen, died at School, Aberdeen, in 1840. [AJ.11.8.1840]

TENNANT, HELEN MILNE, eldest daughter of John Tennant in Aberdeen, widow of George Law, married Robert McFarlane a merchant, in Reddersburg, Orange Free State, South Africa, on 19 April 1862. [AJ.5974]

TENNANT, MARGARET THOMSON, youngest daughter of John Tennant of Broadford Works, Aberdeen, married Thomas Holmes, from Nouitdedacht, Orange Free State, South Africa, in Port Elizabeth, Cape of Good Hope, on 5 March 1862. [AJ.5966]

THOM, ARCHIBALD, a surgeon in Perth, Canada, son and heir of Ann Bodie, wife of Alexander Thom a farmer in Old Aberdeen, 1821. [NRS.S/H]

THOM, BISHOP, was admitted as a gardener burgess of Old Aberdeen on 28 October 1811. [ACA]

THOM, GEORGE, master of the Nestor of Aberdeen from Aberdeen bound for Quebec on 14 March 1822. [NRS.E504.1.29]

THOM, JAMES, a business-man in Nova Scotia and New Brunswick for 40 years, died in Aberdeen in 1834. [NBC.9.8.1834]

THOM, JOHN, master of the Isle of Skye of Aberdeen from Tobermory with passengers bound for Prince Edward Island in 1806. [PAPEI.2702][NRS.E504.35.1]

THOM, JOHN, was admitted as a mason burgess of Old Aberdeen on 3 February 1859. [ACA]

THOM, JOHN, born 1770, a manufacturer, died in Aberdeen in 1836. [AJ.16.7.1836]

THOM, Dr WILLIAM, an advocate in Aberdeen, testament, 1797, Comm. Aberdeen. [NRS]

THOM, WILLIAM, was admitted as a merchant burgess of Old Aberdeen on 25 October 1830. [ACA]

THOM, WILLIAM, son of John Thom an advocate in Aberdeen, was educated at Marischal College in 1848, died when a student. [MCA]

THOMSON, ALEXANDER, born 1790, founder of Geelong, Victoria, Australia, died on 1 January 1866. [Geelong gravestone]

THOMSON, ALEXANDER, a cooper in Aberdeen, died in 1838. [AJ.12.3.1838]

THOMSON, ALEXANDER, a silk mercer in Aberdeen, brother of James Thomson, an agriculturist in County Tyrone, Ireland. [NRS.S/H.1864]

THOMSON, ALEXANDER, from Old Aberdeen, of the Oriental Bank in Victoria, Australia, married Katherine Hooks in Kyneton, Victoria, on 17 August 1876. [AJ.6722]

THOMSON, ANDREW, born 1771, a builder, died at 20 Union Row, Aberdeen, in 1848. [AJ.8.10.1848]

THOMSON, ARTHUR, agent of the Bank of Scotland in Aberdeen in 1849. [POD]

THOMSON, CHRISTIAN RUSSELL, daughter of Robert Thomson a merchant tailor in 40 Broad Street, Aberdeen, married George Coutts, a flax manufacturer in Whangerei, in Auckland, New Zealand, on 8 April 1872. [AJ.6493]

THOMSON, ELIZA, born 1795, daughter of Reverend Dr Thomson in Footdee, Aberdeen, wife of Alexander Mortimer a baker, died in Aberdeen in 1822. [AJ.25.1.1822]

THOMSON, GEORGE, born 1738, settled in Jamaica, died in Aberdeen on 14 May 1823. [SM.91.776]

THOMSON, GEORGE, a bellman in Aberdeen, was admitted as a burgess of Old Aberdeen on 30 September 1830. [ACA]

THOMSON, GEORGE, was admitted as a wright burgess of Old Aberdeen on 30 September 1830. [ACA]

THOMSON, GEORGE, born 1773, a merchant and shipowner, died at Regent Quay, Aberdeen, in 1853. [AJ.28.1.1853]

THOMSON, GEORGE, from Aberdeen, was educated at King's College, Aberdeen, in 1822, later a minister in Macnab, Canada. [KCA]

THOMSON, GEORGE, in Aberdeen, father of John Thomson of Whitefield Hall, Jamaica, in 1839. [NRS.PS3.16.59]

THOMSON, HELEN, daughter of Andrew Thomson of Cranhill an advocate in Aberdeen, died in 1810. [AJ.27.3.1810]

THOMSON, JAMES, cashier to the Commercial Banking Company in Aberdeen, testament, 1800, Comm. Aberdeen. [NRS]

THOMSON, JAMES, son of James Thomson the town sergeant of Aberdeen, was educated at Marischal College from 1745 to 1748, emigrated to Virginia, a tutor at Oakhill, later minister of Leeds, Fauquier County, died in 1812. [AUReview]

THOMSON, JAMES, a merchant in Aberdeen, testament, 1797, Comm. Aberdeen. [NRS]

THOMSON, JAMES, was admitted as a painter burgess of Old Aberdeen on 25 October 1839. [ACA]

THOMSON, JOHN, MD, born 1757, minister of St Clement's, Aberdeen, died there in 1838. [AJ.16.1.1838]

THOMSON, JOHN, jr., was admitted as a burgess of Old Aberdeen on 8 October 1808. [ACA]

THOMSON, JOHN, was admitted as a merchant burgess of Old Aberdeen on 8 October 1808. [ACA]

THOMSON, JOHN, son of John Thomson in Aberdeen, was educated at Marischal College, Aberdeen, around 1815, settled in the West Indies. [MCA]

THOMSON, JOHN, a skipper in Aberdeen, inventory, 1822, Comm. Aberdeen. [NRS]

THOMSON, JOHN, born 1821 in Aberdeen, master of the barque Ellon of London, died at Port Morant, Jamaica, on 8 February 1852. [AJ.7.4.1852]

THOMSON, JOHN A., son of Arthur Thomson a silversmith in Aberdeen, was educated at Marischal College in 1845. [MCA]

THOMSON, JOHN, son of Robert Thomson a merchant in Aberdeen, was educated at Marischal College in 1847, an advocate in Aberdeen in 1856. [MCA]

THOMSON, MARGARET, daughter of Andrew Thomson of Cranhill an advocate in Aberdeen, died in Aberdeen in 1819. [AJ.6.8.1819]

THOMSON WILLIAM, a baillie of Aberdeen, father of William Thomson in Jamaica who died in Philadelphia, Pennsylvania, on 3 July 1801. [AJ.18.11.1801][GC.1601]

THOMSON, WILLIAM, a mariner in Aberdeen, inventory, 1804, Comm. Aberdeen. [NRS]

THOMSON, WILLIAM, an apprentice shipbuilder in Footdee, Aberdeen, was accused of mobbing and rioting in 1813. [NRS.AD14.13.70]

THOMSON, WILLIAM, son of William Thomson a tailor in Aberdeen, graduated MA from Marischal College in 1817, and MD from Edinburgh University in 1827, later a surgeon of the 67th Regiment of Foot. [MCA]

THOMSON, Mrs, born 1759, wife of Reverend Dr Thomson of St Clement's, Aberdeen, died there in1836. [AJ.22.12.1836]

TILLERAY, JOHN, son of John Tilleray a farmer in Aberdeen, was apprenticed to John Lamb, a wright in Aberdeen, from 1789 to 1794. [ACA]

TILLERAY, WILLIAM, a farmer in Aberdeen, testament, 1795, Comm. Aberdeen. [NRS]

TOASH, MARGARET, in Aberdeen, testament, 1794, Comm. Aberdeen. [NRS]

TORRY, JAMES, born 1795, a surgeon, died at 36 Schoolhill, Aberdeen, in 1852. [AJ.12.4.1852]

TOUGH, JOHN, a mariner in Aberdeen, inventory, 1805, Comm. Aberdeen. [NRS]

TOWER, ALEXANDER, son of George Tower a merchant in Aberdeen, was educated at Marischal College, Aberdeen, from 1815 until 1819, graduated MA, later a planter on St Croix, Danish West Indies. [MCA]; son and heir to his father who died on 17 December 1811. [NRS.S/H]

TOWER, GEORGE, born 1761, a magistrate in Aberdeen, died in 1811. [AJ.17.12]

TOWER, JAMES, son of John Tower in Aberdeen, was educated at Marischal College, Aberdeen, from 1774 to 1778, settled in St Thomas in the West Indies, died in Logie Crimond, Aberdeenshire, on 8 May 1818. [MCA][St Nicholas gravestone, Aberdeen]

TOWER, JOHN, formerly in St Croix in the Danish West Indies, died in Aberdeen on 3 April 1799. [St Nicholas gravestone, Aberdeen]

TOWNS, DAVID, was admitted as a merchant burgess of Old Aberdeen on 27 August 1823. [ACA]

TRAILL, JAMES, was admitted as a trade burgess of Old Aberdeen on 27 October 1817. [ACA]

TROUP, ALEXANDER, son of David Troup a merchant in Aberdeen, graduated MA from Marischal College in 1845, later an Episcopal minister in Buckie and in Dollar. [MCA]

TROUP, JAMES, born 1796, a dancing master in Aberdeen, died in 1842. [AJ.29.7.1842]

TROUPE, WILLIAM, born 1822, a clerk, arrived in Kingston, Jamaica, on 11 May 1841 on board the Rob Roy from Aberdeen. [TNA.CO140/33]

TROUP, WILLIAM MILNE, son of David Troup a merchant in Aberdeen, was educated at Marischal College in 1847. [MCA]

TULLOCH, JAMES, master of the Sisters of Aberdeen, from Aberdeen with passengers bound for Quebec, Restigouche, or Chaleur Bay, in 1836, 1837,1838, [AJ]; master of the St Lawrence from Aberdeen to Quebec with passengers in 1842, 1844, 1845, 1847, 1852, 1853, 1854, 1855; master of the Sir William Wallace of Aberdeen from Aberdeen with passengers bound for Quebec in 1839 and 1842; master of the City of Aberdeen from Aberdeen to Quebec in 1858. [AJ]

TULLOCH, JOHN, Professor of Mathematics in King's College, Aberdeen, died in 1851. [AJ.4.5.1851]

TURNER, Mrs EUPHEMIA, widow of Robert Turner of Menie, died in Old Aberdeen in 1823. [AJ.12.10.1823]

TURNER, KEITH, of Turnerhall, born 1767, died in Aberdeen in 1808. [AJ.20.10.1808]

TURNER, THOMAS ANDREW, son of Robert Turner, the Sheriff Substitute of Aberdeen, was apprenticed to Thomas Bannerman, a merchant in Aberdeen, from 1791 to 1795. [ACA]

TURREFF, JAMES, was admitted as a shoemaker burgess of Old Aberdeen on 29 October 1798. [ACA]

UDNY, HELEN, born 1717, widow of Walter Cochrane sometime Depute Town Clerk of Aberdeen, died in 1809. [AJ.4.12.1809]

URQUHART, HECTOR, born 1816, with Margaret Urquhart, born 1813, Daniel Urquhart, born 1837, and Hector Urquhart, born 1840, arrived in Kingston, Jamaica, on 11 May 1841 on board the Rob Roy from Aberdeen. [TNA.CO140/33]

URQUHART, ISABELLA HELEN, widow of Captain William Urquhart of the 30th Regiment, died in Aberdeen in 1806. [AJ.3.6.1806]

URQUHART, JOHN, of Craigston, died in Aberdeen in 1821. [AJ.24.1.1821]

URQUHART, JOHN, son of John Urquhart a druggist in Aberdeen, graduated MA from Marischal College in 1840, and MD from Edinburgh University in 1847, later Coroner of Madras, India. [MCA]

URQUHART, ROBERT, a medical student in Aberdeen, was accused of violating sepulchres in 1812. [NRS.AD14.12.58]

URQUHART, WILLIAM D., MD, from Aberdeen, a member of the medical staff of the Immigrants Hospital on Wards Island, New York, died there on 28 December 1849. [AJ.5325]

VALENTINE, ALEXANDER, was admitted as a merchant burgess of Old Aberdeen on 29 October 1798. [ACA]

VALENTINE, ANDREW, was admitted as a merchant burgess of Old Aberdeen on 27 April 1795. [ACA]

VALENTINE, JAMES, was admitted as a burgess of Old Aberdeen on 8 October 1808. [ACA]

VIAL, Mrs MARGARET, born 1816, daughter of George MacNaughton in Woodside, Aberdeen, died in Hazel Grove, Illinois, on 18 May 1876. [AJ.18.6.1876]

VOLUME, CHRISTIAN, daughter of William Volume a weaver in Old Aberdeen, versus William Black a sailor in Old Aberdeen, a Declarator of Marriage, 1810, [NRS.CC8.6.1388], and a Process of Divorce, 1810. [NRS.CC8.6.1397]

WALKER, ALEXANDER, a merchant in Aberdeen, testament, 1798, Comm. Aberdeen. [NRS]

WALKER, ALEXANDER, born 1756, a farmer in Aberdeen, emigrated aboard the Draper bound for New York on 6 April 1821. [TNA.HO10218]

WALKER, ALEXANDER, was admitted as a merchant burgess of Old Aberdeen on 9 November 1805. [ACA]

WALKER, ALEXANDER, was admitted as a burgess of Old Aberdeen in April 1820. [ACA]

WALKER, ALEXANDER WALES, MD, born 1831, graduated MD from King's College, Aberdeen, on 6 August 1851, late of St Clement's Street, Aberdeen, died in Penambuco, Brazil, on 15 May 1862. [AJ.5971][KCA]

WALKER, CHARLES, MA, born 1823, died at 1 St Nicholas Street, Aberdeen, in 1848. [AJ.7.11.1848]

WALKER, DAVID, bulker of goods and clerk in the shore-dues office, Aberdeen, a victim of crime in 1825. [NRS.JC26.1825.29]

WALKER, D., master of the Hercules of Aberdeen from Aberdeen with passengers to Quebec in 1835 and in 1836. [QM]

WALKER, GEORGE, was admitted as a blacksmith burgess of Old Aberdeen on 25 January 1802. [ACA]

WALKER, GEORGE P., born 1823, a book-keeper, arrived in Kingston, Jamaica, on 11 May 1841 on board the Rob Roy from Aberdeen. [TNA.CO140/33]

WALKER, JAMES, was admitted as a merchant burgess of Old Aberdeen on 13 April 1801. [ACA]

WALKER, JAMES, from Aberdeen, graduated MA from King's College, Aberdeen, in March 1828, later a minister at Clatt. [KCA]

WALKER, JAMES, was admitted as a wine merchant burgess of Old Aberdeen in April 1820. [ACA]

WALKER, JAMES, born 1845 in Aberdeen, a seaman aboard the Polmaise of London, died in Shanghai, China, on 5 January 1864. [AJ.6059]

WALKER, JEAN, widow of Andrew Henderson a physician, and grand-daughter of Sir Alexander Cumming of Culter, died in Constitution Street, Aberdeen, in 1827. [AJ.23.12.1827]

WALKER, JOHN LUMSDEN, son of David Walker a manufacturer in Aberdeen, graduated MA from Marischal College in 1852, later a minister in Glasgow. [MCA]

WALKER, JOHN, on Prince Edward Island, son and heir of John Walker a flax-dresser in Aberdeen, 1853. [NRS.S/H]

WALKER, MARJORY, born 1845, daughter of John Galen MD in Aberdeen, died in St Louis, Missouri, on 16 May 1870. [AJ.8.6.1870]

WALKER, MARY, relict of George Shand, late in Aberdeen, sometime in Demerara, testament, 1793, Comm. Aberdeen. [NRS]

WALKER, PETER, a merchant in Stirling, later in New York, nephew and heir of Robert Walker a merchant in Aberdeen, 1835. [NRS.S/H]

WALKER, WILLIAM, a porter in Aberdeen, testament, 1794, Comm. Aberdeen, [NRS]

WALKER, WILLIAM, was admitted as a merchant burgess of Old Aberdeen on 30 October 1820. [ACA]

WALKER, WILLIAM, master of the Heroine of Aberdeen, from Aberdeen to Quebec with passengers in 1842 and 1847, [Lloyds][BPP]; of the Renown of Aberdeen from Aberdeen bound with passengers for Quebec in 1854, 1855, 1856, 1857, from Aberdeen with passengers bound for St John, New Brunswick, in 1859 and 1860. [AJ]

WALKER, WILLIAM, son of William Walker a merchant in Aberdeen, graduated MA from Marischal College in 1849 and MD in 1855. [MCA]

WALKER, Captain, master of the Hannibal of Aberdeen, from Aberdeen with passengers bound for Sydney, New South Wales, Australia, in February 1854. [AJ.5538]

WALLACE, ALEXANDER, a butcher in Aberdeen, testament, 1795, Comm. Aberdeen. [NRS]

WALLACE, ALEXANDER, son of Alexander Wallace, a butcher in Aberdeen, was apprenticed to James Finnie, a wright in Aberdeen, from 1790 to 1795. [ACA]

WALLACE, HUGH, son of William Wallace a shoemaker in Aberdeen, was educated at Marischal College in 1847, later a minister in Kendal. [MCA]

WARRACK, ROBERT, born 1827, from Aberdeen, died in Detroit, Michigan, on 30 March 1859. [AJ.1.5.1859]

WATSON, ALEXANDER, was admitted as a merchant burgess of Old Aberdeen on 20 February 1824. [ACA]

WATSON, ALEXANDER, son of Alexander Watson a bookseller in Aberdeen, a soldier of the 46th Regiment, died in Barbados on 10 December 1842. [AJ.4968]

WATSON, JAMES, an advocate in Aberdeen, testaments, 1797-1798, Comm. Aberdeen. [NRS]

WATSON, JAMES, a master mariner in Aberdeen, inventory, 1808, Comm. Aberdeen. [NRS]

WATSON, JAMES, born 1815 in Aberdeen, emigrated to Australia in 1840, died at Midden Point, Murray River, Port Philip, Victoria, Australia, on 6 June 1850. [AJ.5368]

WATSON, JOHN, an advocate, died in Aberdeen in 1832. [AJ.24.4.1832]

WATSON, MARY, born 1800, daughter of Robert Watson a manufacturer in Stoneywood, and wife of William Leslie an architect in Aberdeen, died at 8 Golden Square, Aberdeen, in 1853. [AJ.21.7.1853]

WATSON, ROBERT, in Aberdeen, was apprenticed to Margaret Morice, a baker in Aberdeen, from 1786 to 1791. [ACA]

WATSON, ROBERT, in Aberdeen, died 21 February 1849, father of John Watson a hotel keeper in Brisbane, Queensland, Australia. [NRS.S/H]

WATSON, ROBERT, in Victoria, Vancouver Island, Canada, son and heir of Robert Watson a merchant in Aberdeen who died on 21 February 1849. [NRS.S/H]

WATSON, WILLIAM, son of William Watson in Aberdeen, graduated MA in 1846 and MB in 1853 from Marischal College. [MCA]

WATT, ALEXANDER, born 1772, a land surveyor, died in Aberdeen in 1850. [AJ.20.4.1850]

WATT, ALEXANDER, was admitted as a blacksmith burgess of Old Aberdeen on 27 October 1800. [ACA]

WATT, A., master of the Emperor Alexander of Aberdeen trading with Quebec in 1823, 1824. [QM][MG]

WATT, ELIZABETH, daughter of Reverend James Watt of Aberdeen Grammar School, married Alexander Hutchison a Writer to the Signet in Cape Town, South Africa, there on 19 June 1851. [W.1252]

WATT, GEORGE, born 1763, a surgeon, died in Aberdeen in 1839. [AJ.10.7.1839]

WATT, JOHN, was admitted as a burgess of Old Aberdeen on 8 October 1808. [ACA]

WATT, PATRICK, a vintner in Aberdeen, testament, 1791, Comm. Aberdeen. [NRS]

WATT, ROBERT LESLIE, born 1789, a shoemaker from Aberdeen, died in Scranton, Pennsylvania, on 9 August 1859. [AJ.5.10.1859]

WATT, WILLIAM, was admitted as a merchant burgess of Old Aberdeen on 8 October 1808. [ACA]

WATT, WILLIAM, was admitted as a merchant burgess of Old Aberdeen on 27 November 1824. [ACA]

WEBSTER, ALEXANDER, a writer in Aberdeen, son of John Webster a manufacturer in Aberdeen, was admitted as a Notary Public on 11 July 1794, died 26 March 1855. [NRS.NP2.35.189]

WEBSTER, ALEXANDER, son of William Webster a baker in Aberdeen, graduated MA from Marischal College in 1849, a minister in Kilmarnock and Edinburgh. [MCA]

WEBSTER, ALEXANDER, born 1852, died in South Africa on 17 June 1913. [St Clement's gravestone, Aberdeen]

WEBSTER, ANDREW, was admitted as a weaver burgess of Old Aberdeen on 26 October 1801. [ACA]

WEBSTER, CATHERINE, wife of C. Winchester in Aberdeen, sister and heir of James Webster of Content Estate, Jamaica, in 1827. [NRS.S/H]

WEBSTER, CHARLES, from Aberdeen, arrived in New York in June 1838 on the St Andrew from Liverpool. [MacG.1.5]

WEBSTER, DONALD, was admitted as a trade burgess of Old Aberdeen on 30 October 1820. [ACA]

WEBSTER, JAMES, married Margaretta Sophia Gray, daughter of William Gray a printer in Montreal, Quebec, in Aberdeen on 26 February 1832. [AJ.4386]

WEBSTER, JOHN, born 1742, a convenor, died in Aberdeen in 1826. [AJ.8.4.1826]

WEDDERBURN, ALEXANDER, born 1796 in Aberdeen, Chief Emigration Agent for New Brunswick, died in St John, NB, on 17 June 1843. [NBC24.6.1843]

WEIR, WILLIAM, born 1797, master of the barque Anasta of Aberdeen, died at the Cape of Good Hope, South Africa, in January 1848. [AJ.5234]

WELSH, ROBERT, a shipmaster in Aberdeen, inventory, 1805, Comm. Aberdeen. [NRS]

WESTLAND, JOHN, born 1834, a stonecutter from Aberdeen, settled in Quincy, Massachusetts, in 1869, died in Boston on 10 July 1872. [AJ.9500]

WHITE, ADAM, son of William White a merchant in Aberdeen, graduated MA from Marischal College in 1846, a missionary in India. [MCA]

WHITE, Mrs ELIZABETH, wife of David White a tailor in Jamaica, sister and heir of Jean and Margaret Gray, daughters of William Gray a merchant in Aberdeen, in 1793. [NRS.S/H]

WHITE, JOHN FORBES, son of William White a grain merchant in Aberdeen, graduated MA from Marischal College in 1844, a merchant in Aberdeen and Dundee. [MCA]

WHITE, ROBERT, son of James White an architect in Aberdeen, graduated MA from Marischal College in 1840. [MCA]

WIGHT, JOHN, was admitted as a butcher burgess of Old Aberdeen, on 22 April 1811. [ACA]

WILDGOOSE, ALEXANDER, born 1778 in Aberdeen, a master builder in the Bahamas for 20 years, died on 3 July 1810. [Bahamas Royal Gazette, 4.7.1810]

WILDGOOSE, JAMES, born 1727, son of John Wildgoose in Old Deer, was apprenticed to Colin Allan a goldsmith in Aberdeen from 1749 to 1756, later a silversmith in Aberdeen who was buried in St Peter's, Aberdeen, on 4 November 1795. [AU.ms2459]

WILDGOOSE, JOHN, at Bridge of Don, was admitted as a trade burgess of Old Aberdeen on 30 October 1815. [ACA]

WILDGOOSE, JOHN, jr, at Bridge of Don, was admitted as a trade burgess of Old Aberdeen on 30 October 1815. [ACA]

WILKINSON, WILLIAM, graduated MA from Cambridge University in 1806, Episcopal minister of St Paul's, Aberdeen, from 1809 until 1822.

WILL, GEORGE, was admitted as a trade burgess of Old Aberdeen in September 1812. [ACA]

WILL, JAMES, was admitted as a weaver burgess of Old Aberdeen on 2 April 1828. [ACA]

WILL, JOHN HADDEN, son of Thomas Will a merchant in Aberdeen, was educated at Marischal College in 1846, a manufacturer's agent in London. [MCA]

WILL, ROBERT, was admitted as a carter burgess of Old Aberdeen on 1 October 1810. [ACA]

WILLIAMS, CHARLES, son of James Williams in Aberdeen, was educated at Marischal College in 1842. [MCA]

WILLIAMSON, ALEXANDER, son of Benjamin Williamson MD in Aberdeen was educated at Marischal College in 1842, joined the merchant navy. [MCA]

WILLIAMSON, BENJAMIN, MD, born 1789, died at 239 Union Street West, Aberdeen, in 1850. [AJ.23.8.1850]

WILLIAMSON, BENJAMIN, son of Benjamin Williamson MD in Aberdeen was educated at Marischal College in 1848, graduated MB in 1854. [MCA]

WILLIAMSON, HARVEY, son of Peter Williamson a druggist in Aberdeen, was educated at Marischal College in 1842, later a druggist in Aberdeen. [MCA]

WILLIAMSON, HENRY, son of Benjamin Williamson MD in Aberdeen was educated at Marischal College in 1844. [MCA]

WILLIAMSON, WILLIAM, son of Benjamin Williamson MD in Aberdeen was educated at Marischal College in 1840, graduated MA, later MD from Edinburgh University in 1847. [MCA]

WILLOX, ALEXANDER, a smith in Aberdeen, applied to settle in Canada in 1815. [NRS.RH9]

WILLOX, GEORGE, a merchant in Old Aberdeen, testament, 1800, Comm. Aberdeen. [NRS]

WILLOX, THOMAS, mariner on the Ariadne of Aberdeen testament, 1800, Comm Aberdeen. [NRS]

WILSON, ARTHUR, was admitted as a merchant burgess of Old Aberdeen in April 1812. [ACA]

WILSON, DAVID, a builder in Aberdeen, died in 1838, father of George Wilson in Melbourne, Victoria, Australia. [NRS.S/H]

WILSON, JAMES, born 1811, arrived in Kingston, Jamaica, on 11 May 1841 on board the Rob Roy from Aberdeen. [TNA.CO140/33]

WILSON, JAMES HALL, son of Thomas Wilson a cooper in Aberdeen, was educated at Marischal College in 1850s, later a Congregationalist minister in Aberdeen, graduated Doctor of Divinity at Waynesburg College in USA in 1880. [MCA]

WILSON, MARGARET, relict of David Rattray a confectioner in Aberdeen, testament, 1794, Comm. Aberdeen. [NRS]

WILSON, NATHANIEL, a writer in Aberdeen, witnessed a deed in Aberdeen on 7 March 1807. [NRS.RD5.271.168]

WILSON, WILLIAM, was admitted as a trade burgess of Old Aberdeen in October 1816. [ACA] in 1842, a minister in Malta. [MCA]

WILSON, WILLIAM, from Aberdeen, was educated at Marischal College in 1849, a minister in Musselburgh. [MCA]

WISELY, GEORGE, son of George Wisely a merchant in Aberdeen, graduated MA from Marischal College in 1846, later a minister in Malta. [MCA]

WISHART, DANIEL, from Aberdeen, chief mate of the barque John King of Glasgow, died in Jamaica on 28 September 1857. [AJ.6.1.1858]

WISHART, ISOBEL, spouse to Robert McCombie a merchant in Aberdeen, died there in 1800. [AJ.31.3.1800]

WISHART, JEAN, in Aberdeen, testament, 1791, Comm. Aberdeen. [NRS]

WISHART, ROBERT, born 1747, a tailor and Convenor of the Incorporated Trades of Old Aberdeen, died at 99 Spital, Aberdeen, in 1841. [AJ.2.11.1841]

WRIGHT, PATRICK R., from Aberdeen, married Mary Anne Chapman from Yorkshire, in Coburg, Canada, on 4 March 1846. [AJ.5133]

WOOD, HELEN, born 1801, widow of William Hughes a shoemaker in Gallowgate, Aberdeen, was accused of uttering forged notes in 1824. [NRS.AD14.24.89]

WOOD, JAMES, was admitted as a burgess of Old Aberdeen on 8 October 1808. [ACA]

WOOD, JAMES, eldest son of Robert Wood in Aberdeen, died in Nieman, Baringhurst, Victoria, Australia, on 29 December 1871. [AJ.6477]

WOOD, JOHN, son of Joseph Wood a shoemaker in Aberdeen, a student at Marischal College in 1820s, was admitted as a Member of the Royal College of Surgeons in 1828, in the Service of the East India Company. [MCA]

WOOD, WILLIAM, was admitted as a merchant burgess of Old Aberdeen on 14 November 1799. [ACA]

WRIGHT, PATRICK R., from Aberdeen, married Mary Anne Chapman from Yorkshire, in Coburg, Canada, on 4 March 1846. [AJ.5133]

WYLIE, D., cashier of the Aberdeen Bank in 1849. [POD]

YATES, ANDREW, born 1776 in Aberdeen, died 25 January 1804, buried at Old Fourth Creek, Statesville, Iredell County, North Carolina. [Statesville gravestone]

YEATS, ALEXANDER, son of George Yeats a merchant in Aberdeen, graduated MA from Marischal College in 1847, an advocate in Aberdeen in 1860. [MCA]

YOUNG, GEORGE, born 1835, from Aberdeen, died in Montreal, Quebec, on 13 March 1861. [AJ.5909]

YOUNG, GEORGE, born 1822, seventh son of James Young in , Rotterdam former Provost of Aberdeen, died in Torrens Park, Adelaide, South Australia, on 29 April 1869. [AJ.6341]

YOUNG, JANE, born 1813, daughter of James Young in Rotterdam and sometime Provost of Aberdeen, was drowned near Aberdeen in 1828. [AJ.26.6.1828]

YOUNG, JOHN, a physician in Montserrat, British West Indies, nephew and heir of Rebecca Gibbon or Fraser or Mearns in Aberdeen, widow of John Fraser a merchant in Aberdeen in 1792. [NRS.S/H]

YOUNG, THOMAS HALLIDAY, son of James Young in Aberdeen, was educated at Marischal College in 1840. [MCA]

YOUNG, WILLIAM, born 1736, died in Aberdeen in 1814. [AJ.28.11.1814]

YOUNGSON, JANET, born 1717, died in Aberdeen in 1818. [AJ.28.6.1818]

YULE, ALEXANDER, master of the Ploughman of Aberdeen from Aberdeen with passengers bound for Pictou, Nova Scotia, in 1811. [NRS.E504.1.24]

YULE, JESSIE, born 1836, daughter of Alexander Gibson in Aberdeen, died in Kenosha, Wisconsin, on 23 June 1854. [AJ.18.10.1854]

www.ingramcontent.com/pod-product-compliance
Lightning Source LLC
Chambersburg PA
CBHW052100230426
43662CB00036B/1709